CUSTOMER
INTIMACY

CUSTOMER INTIMACY

Pick Your Partners,
Shape Your Culture,
Win Together

FRED WIERSEMA

HarperCollinsBusiness
A division of HarperCollins*Publishers*

HarperCollins*Publishers*
77–85 Fulham Palace Road,
Hammersmith, London W6 8JB

Published by HarperCollins*Publishers* 1997
1 3 5 7 9 8 6 4 2

First published in the USA by
Knowledge Exchange 1996

A catalogue record for this book
is available from the British Library

ISBN 0 00 255821 1

Set in Bembo

Printed and bound by
Caledonian Book Manufacturing Ltd, Glasgow

To Catherine and Annelise,
whose cheer and affection
I treasure forever

CONTENTS

PART I

Why Customer Intimacy Now?

1 | CUSTOMER INTIMACY — WHAT IT IS AND WHY IT WINS

Just how intimate can you get?

Imagine a company that sells a commodity product and then dispatches trained teams to its customers' factories worldwide to teach them how to use less of it.

Counterintuitive?

Absolutely.

Worth it?

By focusing on customer performance as its real product, GE Plastics has become an industry leader and claims an expanding market share. The Pittsfield, Massachusetts–based division of giant General Electric Company assembles industry-specific teams that help customers develop new products and process technologies, and design manufacturing processes, that keep costs low and performance high. They also send follow-up teams to uncover problems in customers' plants. Too much scrap? Trouble with yield or inventory turns? The GE Plastics performance team works side by side with its customers to design solutions, and put them into practice.

Results? GE Plastics' productivity program saved its customers more than $68 million in 1995 alone while GE Plastics experienced an 11 percent increase in revenue.

Just how intimate can you get?

Imagine a company that sends its executives into its customers' basement workshops to watch over their shoulders and then to trail them to the hardware store.

Expensive?

Very.

Productive?

By learning what its customers really want for their projects, toolmaker Black & Decker recaptured its flagging do-it-yourself market, fighting back strong challenges from Makita and Sears. Like anthropologists, B&D marketing executives studied 50 male home-owners—ages 25 to 54—as they used power tools to work on projects. The executives aimed to discover exactly why users favored certain tools over others. Dissatisfaction was high. Do-it-yourselfers wanted a cordless drill with enough power to complete a good-sized job. They wanted sanders and circular saws that didn't kick up clouds of sawdust; safety mechanisms that would instantly stop saw blades from spinning when they switched off power; a hotline for questions about home-repair problems. Never before had customers so clearly voiced their concerns.

Results? Do-it-yourselfers got equipment that matched their wants: B&D introduced its Quantum line of saws, drills, and small power tools, priced from $50 to $120. The market responded quickly: Introduced late in 1993, by the end of 1994, Quantum surpassed its sales goal and was already upgrading its tools to QuantumPro.

Just how intimate can you get?

Imagine a small company—with hundreds of customers—that fires all but the toughest of them.

Risky?

Absolutely.

Rewarding?

By focusing on a few stretch customers, Nypro, Inc., a Clinton, Massachusetts–based plastics-injection molder, transformed itself from an undistinguished also-ran to an internationally heralded leader in zero-defect production. Nypro searched out sophisticated customers, initially targeting cutting-edge manufacturers of health-care products whose needs for product safety demanded far higher specifications than any existing injection process could deliver. Nypro designed new injection processes for each customer, sharing insights with the customers' own engineering and marketing teams to solve their specific problems. They worked together: partners in the search for innovation. Nypro situated its new plants next door to its customers and integrated its new process with theirs.

Results? Nypro's customers got more sophisticated products produced at lower cost with a faster cycle time and fewer defects. For its part, Nypro saw annual net income rise from less than $1 million on sales of $50 million to nearly $13 million on sales of $197 million, in less than a decade.

GE Plastics, Black & Decker, and Nypro: What these three companies have in common—beyond their impressive success—is their dedication to their customers' results. Like scores of today's like-minded market leaders around the world, they are on the cutting edge of the most important strategic transformation of the decade: the shift to customer intimacy. They've abandoned the old us-versus-them mind-set to embrace a single common insight: The largest source of growth, advantage, and profit resides in the design and development of intimacy with customers.

Customer-intimate companies come in many shapes and sizes. Some, like Microsoft Corporation, CIGNA Corporation, and Baxter International Inc., are large. Other emerging leaders, companies like Calyx & Corolla and Bollinger Industries, are small. Some are American household names: Levi Strauss Associates and Staples National Advantage. Others, like Scania, the Swedish truck and bus manufacturer, and Sumitomo Forestry, the Japanese construction giant, are international stars. But whatever product or service they sell, they are all in the business of creating new value for their customers.

Customer intimacy doesn't call for increasing customer satisfaction. It requires taking responsibility for customers' results. It doesn't impose arm's length goodwill. It requires down-in-the-trenches solidarity, the exchange of useful information, and the cooperative pursuit of results.

My research shows that about one in three market-leading companies across the spectrum of industries attains prominence today by making the most of practices I call customer intimate. That same research indicates that those practices are spreading rapidly. Why? Because managers and executives can see that they work, and they want to reap the rewards themselves.

But are those companies merely baby-sitting their customers? Aren't they blurring real and useful distinctions between supplier and buyer? Don't they encourage their customers to enter into an unhealthy dependency?

No, no, and no.

Rather than simply react to their customers' every whim, customer-intimate suppliers discover how to provide complete solutions to customers' needs. In doing so, they become indispensable partners, often merging their operations with those of their customers. They take a major stake in their customers' ultimate successes.

They don't blur distinctions—in fact, they create new and

sharper ones. When two organizations move from a simple supply-and-buy relationship to the technical and operational complexities of a customer-intimate relationship, the unique responsibilities of each become unmistakable. They develop a new mind-set—a new way of doing business—with new structures, new strategies, new values, and a new vision.

Like GE Plastics, other customer-intimate suppliers know that customer performance is the name of the game. And that emanates from sharing information and building trust. Like Black & Decker, they see their customers' problems as their own, and know that customer intimacy is the best way to create hard, tangible, rewarding results for both sides. Like Nypro, they're picky about their customers, and they're willing to engage in truly cooperative partnerships with the customers they do choose.

ACTIONS, NOT ACCIDENTS

Customer-intimate companies bring an entirely fresh perspective. They discover unsuspected problems, detect unrealized potential, and create a dynamic synergy with customers. In the integration of their operations, suppliers become more than merely useful: They become indispensable.

The suppliers who lead today's markets are those that constantly think about their customers. They analyze their systems, recognize their flaws, challenge their assumptions, and assume responsibility for initiating change. In this transformed market, what counts is the human dimension. Customer-intimate companies craft relationships of openness and confidence with wit and skill. Customer intimacy calls for a company's total response. It calls for a discipline that summons the full force of a company's creative imagination: heroic performances from service staffs, resourceful use of information technology to speed up partnering interactions, and continual readiness to anticipate both trouble and opportunity in customers' futures. All these factors combine to redraw traditional boundaries between a company and its customers or clients. But in an organization's search for total solutions, it will find that the most important determinants of success are imagination and the special insight it gives into customers' needs—recognized and unrecognized.

Microsoft's astounding worldwide success is deeply rooted in its commitment to search for, shape, and satisfy customer needs. Consider how far Eric LeVine, program manager for Word, Microsoft's word-processing software, went to get results for his customers.

When Microsoft started to get complaints about Word 6.0, LeVine didn't hesitate to address them. He noticed a common thread: Certain of the package's functions—paragraph numbering, cross-referencing, and the like—were causing problems for law offices, which constituted a significant segment of the market for word-processing software. "I went to my boss," LeVine says, "and told him that I was tired of hearing these bits of noise. I said to him, I'm going out there to study the legal market to figure out exactly what we need to do to keep those guys happy."

For one hellish month, LeVine crisscrossed the country on planes, trains, and long-distance phone lines. He visited 35 firms and watched attorneys, information systems staff, and legal secretaries as they worked, and he carefully noted their every keystroke.

LeVine's attentiveness paid off: He was able to distinguish between the users' implementation problems and weaknesses in the software itself. More to the point, having observed his customers so closely, LeVine learned to recognize the origins of their problems, and that enabled him to move toward workable solutions he could incorporate into the software.

"It was a matter of examining all the little pieces and tying together all the loose ends," says LeVine. "But before I went and started talking to people, I didn't even know what all the little pieces were. I knew if we did it right, everyone would end up winning."

That's customer intimacy in action: Deliver it right, and supplier and customer win together.

Like Microsoft, Kennametal, Inc., a $1-billion metal-cutting tools manufacturer, focuses on delivering the best result. As *Fortune* magazine recounted in a story on the company, Kennametal doesn't sell cutting tools to its customers, it sells cutting-tool performance for its customers. In some cases, this requires Kennametal to integrate functions, manage its customers' inventory or observe its customers' other tools as they are tested against Kennametal products. If Kennametal discovers during those processes that its competitor's product will do a job better at that particular point in time, that's the tool Kennametal recommends: whatever gives the best result. This motivates Kennametal to continuously improve its own products, and it simultaneously strengthens its position against the competition as a total-solution provider. Kennametal isn't a vendor. It's a partner: The best result for their customer is the best result for them.

Delivering on that partnership takes more than a promise in a sales pitch. Indeed, according to James Heaton, Kennametal's director of customer satisfaction, the sales force is sometimes a barrier to intimacy. "Buyers and sellers focus on what they see as the driving issue—price—and frequently ignore the more complex and subtle issues: quality, performance, cost of use, and mutual understanding," he explains.

Determined to broaden avenues of communication, Heaton began bussing a cross section of Kennametal employees to customers' plants. In one instance, he sent 300 employees selected from every level of Kennametal's factory in Johnson City, Tennessee, to the Dana Corporation auto-parts manufacturing plant in Bristol, Virginia. There, Kennametal employees saw the conditions under which people use their tools, as well as the mayhem that can result when those tools fail.

Like Eric LeVine's travels, Kennametal's peregrinations yielded practical knowledge that the company applied to every stage of the manufacturing and sales processes. And Kennametal's investment of time, energy, and money delivered a clear message to its customers: The company is committed to performance and mutual benefit.

That commitment, and the results it delivers, change entire markets. As more and more customers experience exceptional performance—whatever it takes to solve their problems—fewer and fewer will settle for anything less.

THE EXPECTATIONS GAP

You don't have to look far to spot the unmet needs of customers today. They are everywhere: in products and services that weren't carefully designed and therefore fall far short of their potential.

➤ Think about all the underutilized VCRs and personal computers. Like many other consumers, I don't know how to program my VCR. On many of the technologically advanced products I own, I don't know which buttons I should push to make my life easier and more productive. How many consumers over the age of 20 know how to take advantage of sophisticated software?

➤ Look at handheld vacuums. Most of them are so inefficient they sit collecting more dust than they'll ever pick up. Most home exercise machines are so complicated they're featured at every suburban garage sale you drive past. And vegetable juicers are so hard to clean and reassemble they've given carrot juice a bad name. Most of those white elephants started life as brilliant ideas. They ultimately failed as products because no one did the extra legwork necessary to anticipate the full spectrum of customer needs.

➤ Consider an office that invests in an expensive cutting-edge information system. After disappointing delays and hefty cost overruns, the foolish system barely does what it's supposed to, and by the time it's fully operational it's already laughably obsolete.

➤ Or reflect, in a broader commercial context, on the waste from underutilized machines or unproductive workers. Performance is more important than ever before, but all too often the goods and services customers buy don't deliver.

All those are instances of what I call the expectations gap. Customers either don't get what they need, or they get what they don't need.

Customer-intimate companies start by addressing that gap. They become expert at revealing and articulating those mismatches, and they fashion comprehensive solutions to fix them. They see the world through their customers' eyes, and they understand their customers' points of view. But because they bring an outsider's perspective, they often see things the customer overlooks. A company immersed in its day-to-day workings often can't pinpoint its problems, while a supplier with a fresh eye—and a stake in the company's productivity—can spot them immediately. Such customer-intimate suppliers provide products and services that address the sources of their customers' real problems rather than their immediate symptoms.

But customer-intimate companies don't stop there. The knowledge generated in fixing one problem helps them to anticipate future difficulties. Like the waiter who unobtrusively refills your glass before you are even aware that it's empty, they deal with the future as well as the present.

Customer intimacy is more than being customer-driven and sensitive to customers' every demand. Customer-intimate companies seek solutions that exceed immediate needs and demands. They open commercial opportunities for their customers and for themselves by actualizing unrealized potential and forestalling problems. They push the traditional boundaries until they find and deliver the best total solution for each and every client.

They know they have no alternative—and no greater opportunity.

THE SEARCH FOR VALUE

It has been a doleful business truth for more than two decades: Customers grow ever more demanding, and suppliers must change just to keep up. They must add ever greater value to the products and services they sell. In the 1970s and early 1980s many companies had to admit that they didn't know how to make durable goods or deliver reliable services. Defect rates as high as 20 or 30 percent were common, and apathetic service was the norm. "It won't work, and nobody cares," cynical customers lamented. But a few enlightened companies decided they could win customers' hearts by offering sound brand-name products, reliable services, and solid dependability. These companies moved to market leadership and raised the level of customer expectation.

They initiated Stage One of the quest for value: The search for ways to meet increasingly aggressive customer demands. A generation of managers worked to erase quality problems, improve consistency, and aim for zero-defect operations—first in Japan and later in the United States and other countries. The buzz of Total Quality and all its variants filled the air. Companies learned to operate in a continuous-improvement mode, turning state-of-the-art into standard operating procedure. U.S. companies that starred in those efforts—Federal Express, Motorola, Xerox—saw their superior performance rewarded in the marketplace. Everyone wanted a chance at the coveted Malcolm Baldrige Award.

The results were heartening. Customers could buy a Detroit-made car with confidence that it wouldn't break down after 10,000 miles. They could direct dial Beijing with confidence that their call would go right through. Good functioning became the norm. But rather than satisfy customer hunger, it only increased value-whetted appetites for more convenience, lower prices, and an endless stream of innovative products and services.

Suppliers had to find new ways to keep up.

So began Stage Two, the heyday of reengineering. Audacious managers radically redesigned business processes, and boosted their ability to meet customers' escalating appetites. Wasteful activities were excised, costs lowered. Product development accelerated and proliferated, creating entirely new markets and new needs.

In that era, managers learned to focus their operations: They leveraged their core business processes rather than trying to make improvements across the board. Some of those managers were guided by *The Discipline of Market Leaders,* a book that I coauthored with Michael Treacy. In that book, which was based on five years of research and the experiences of 80 market-leading firms, we asserted that successful organizations excel at delivering one type of value to their chosen customers. That is, their managers focus on a single value discipline—best total cost, best product, or best total solution—and build their organization around it.

Choosing one discipline does not mean abandoning the others. It means that a company directs its energy and emphasis: Going for the gold in their chosen discipline and settling for a silver or bronze in the others. Narrow your focus, we said, if you aspire to be a market leader. A jack of all trades ends up master of none.

AT&T understood that principle when it decided to break itself into three businesses, each focusing on meeting the brutal demands of its respective marketplace. So did Xerox, General Dynamics, and many other companies that decided to outsource, or subcontract, information systems and noncritical business processes. Both outsourcer and supplier benefited from their narrower focus.

Today, the quest for value creation is entering Stage Three: the shift to customer intimacy. Customers continue to raise the level of their requirements, but their range extends beyond best price and best product. Now, more than ever, customers hunger for results—superior results—from the products they use. And customer intimacy gives it to them.

Customers have evermore complicated and specific ideas of what "results" should mean. It might mean that the outsourced payroll system is timely and that it can accommodate unique specifications. It might mean the customer can buy a custom drill-bit set rather than having to buy 16 bits to get the 6 he wants. It might mean being allowed to board a flight even after losing a ticket—and expecting the airline to have the electronic systems to make it possible.

Today's customers want exactly the right selection of products or services that will help them get exactly the total solution they have in mind.

Customers refuse to be anonymous. Forget about trying to satisfy them with generic treatment or standard service—no matter how flawless. Don't even think of offering one-size-fits-all products—no matter how technologically brilliant. And they have no tolerance for the supplier who shakes hands and disappears after the sale. Don't expect to get away with a good-luck-you're-on-your-own attitude. Nobody's buying it anymore.

The problem is that although many companies hear the swelling chorus of demands, they cannot, try as they may, respond properly. Yes, they've eliminated inefficiencies and instilled quality thinking. Those reforms raised their across-the-board conditioning and established a platform for ongoing improvement. Yes, they've focused their operations and reengineered their business processes to win the specific race. Now they offer the best product or best price or most convenience.

But the key move—learning to custom-design their businesses imaginatively and irresistibly—eludes them. Maybe they're unable to reorient their cultures toward values of sharing and trust: Such terminology is enough to make certain traditional managers gag. Perhaps they're unable even to pick clients that deserve the kind of service-collaboration a customer-intimate company can offer. Or perhaps their difficulty is technological: With information systems designed for a different era, they lack the kind of customer data that permit fine-tuning for superior value and results. Or maybe they just can't bring themselves to share the costs and benefits of customer intimacy in a fair and equitable manner: Their model of engagement always requires a winner and a loser.

That's quite a bundle of challenges to overcome. But managers around the world know they must confront them head on. In 1995 CSC/Index, the international management-consulting firm, canvassed 400 European and American companies in a wide range of industries. Three out of four presidents, CEOs, and senior executives put the quest for "more complete solutions" at the top of their competitive agenda. Delivering the "best customized fit" ranked as the third most important concern in addressing rising customer expectations. Those are the strengths of customer intimacy. ("Lower prices" ranked second.)

Is customer intimacy worth the trouble? The companies I have featured in this book are committed to it, and their successes support that commitment. They are pioneers in a growth market for individualized results—transforming themselves, their customers, and their markets as they move forward to raise the competitive bar. Such companies as Home Depot, USAA, High Point Chemical, Reynolds Metals, British Airways, Germany's Breuninger department stores, Bank of Ireland, and Air Liquide in France have all seen the future, and they have devised a strategy to capture it. Even IBM is staking its success—once again—on becoming the superior total-solutions provider in its field.

IS CUSTOMER INTIMACY FOR YOU?

In the chapters that follow we'll look at a broad variety of innovative practitioners of intimacy: companies large and small, domestic and international, from consumer retailers to business-to-business suppliers of all kinds of goods and services. We'll see how they designed their operating models and developed the skills to execute them. We'll look at how they initiated their shift to intimacy, and at the pitfalls they faced as they moved forward. We'll explore how they learned to choose and engage customers and how to build the no-surprises confidence that makes collaboration grow. And we'll see how they shaped their own cultures, aligned everyone to the same goal, and created new measurement systems and management structures to support them.

Who Is Customer Intimacy For?

It is for any manager who is searching for a competitive leg up.

➤ Customer intimacy is for executives and managers in small and entrepreneurial businesses—companies that compete against rivals with vastly superior resources, scale advantages, or R&D skills. Many resource-shallow contenders are instinctively customer intimate. The discipline of operational excellence—offering the best total cost—comes naturally to heavyweights like Wal-Mart Stores, Inc. or Dow Chemical Company. And product leadership—providing the best product—is naturally the preferred option for creative engines like AT&T's Bell Labs or 3M. Customer intimacy provides a way for the rest of us to compete. Witness how the comparatively resource-poor Airborne Freight Corporation carved out a niche against package-delivery titans Federal Express Corporation and United Parcel Service; how contract chip manufacturer Solectron Corporation thrives in the shadow of Intel Corporation by designing chip configurations that suit the special needs of its customers' computers; or how such independent booksellers as The Tattered Cover Bookstore in Denver and R.J. Julia Booksellers in Madison, Connecticut, prosper in markets dogged by superstores and bookseller chains.

➤ Even for the large or resource rich, customer intimacy may be the surest path to enduring success. It works for Microsoft, as we saw earlier in this chapter, and it works for Levi Strauss. Indeed, for some large companies customer intimacy may well be the only option for part of their business, or even their entire operation. Despite its size and decades of experience, Sears, for example, has little chance of gaining on Wal-Mart, which dominates the operational-excellence track, or of overtaking The Gap as a fashion tastemaker and product leader. Customer intimacy offers the best possible zone of advantage.

➤ Customer intimacy is for executives and managers who have hit the self-improvement wall. After years and years of TQMing and reengineering, they have slashed costs, defect rates, and response times impressively. But so have their rivals. Customer intimacy is the only way to distinguish themselves. In the fiercely competitive long-distance telephone service industry, for example, a company like Cable & Wireless Inc. (CWI) can point with justifiable pride to its 98 percent customer-retention rate, but, since most of the competition can claim a 96 or 97 percent customer-retention rate, CWI's retention isn't its only selling point. Instead CWI sells and delivers intimacy, accuracy, low defect rate, and rapid turnaround time that customers truly prize.

Who Inside Such a Company Must Practice Customer Intimacy?

Everyone, from the front line to the back office, the executive suite to the loading dock. Customer intimacy gives senior managers a new vision of the future, a strategy that makes sense, and the tactics to make it work. It helps sales and account managers build deeper and more productive relationships with selected customers, arming them with a real-world model of success in their often lonely battle to unite factory and field. Customer intimacy helps information-technology professionals leverage emerging innovation: keeping information flowing back and forth to customers, and coaching them on how to get the best results with that information. Customer intimacy will help human-resource professionals, too, as they move to integrate the supplier's personnel into a customer's operation—a most sensitive challenge of the commitment to deliver results.

Bottom line? There are two main reasons to read this book.

One, it presents an eminently timely and practical way to expand your zone of advantage.

And two, your competitors may already be halfway through the next chapter.

2 | THE ILLUSION OF SATISFACTION

Wait a minute, you say. Since the dawn of commerce, haven't entrepreneurs declared their love for their customers? The Phoenicians, I'm sure, swore undying devotion to the barbarians on the coast of Spain to whom they sold bronze axe heads. Who knows, maybe they even offered a money-back guarantee if the axes didn't split wood—or skulls—to the customer's satisfaction.

Today, too, it would be difficult to find a company that doesn't proudly claim to be a customer-oriented, customer-focused, or even customer-driven enterprise. But look a little closer at how those companies put their assertions into practice, and often you discover an array of notions and assumptions that range from superficial and incomplete to misguided. One company's CEO believes that because he gives his direct phone number to certain valued customers, he's done his job. Another company's managers believe that because they conduct market surveys and focus groups, they know all there is to know about their customers. The executives of still another corporation pat themselves on the back because they invest in smile buttons, awareness programs for employees, and annual reports that sport customers' pictures on the cover.

It's easy to dismiss such rituals as insubstantial, but simple dismissal misses my point. Their approaches differ only in degree from such promise-heavy concepts as relationship selling, loyalty campaigns, and solutions marketing. All of them are well intentioned, but all of them offer, at best, partial solutions to their customers' problems. All found form in a faith in the grail of customer satisfaction, and all, as a result, fall short.

Customer intimacy, as we shall see, begins with a different faith: It starts with a commitment to deliver the best result to each customer. That's why it works.

THE SATISFACTION TRAP

There is nothing wrong with the notion of customer satisfaction per se: Like health, happiness, or profit, it's a concept easy to endorse. The problem comes with its pursuit, which is fraught with peril. Most plans to improve customer satisfaction stand on two shaky—and dangerous—assumptions. The first is that there is a reliable way to measure customer satisfaction or even to agree on what it means. The second is that, once agreed upon, those measurements provide a company with guidance and direction. Both are half-truths at best. And two half-truths don't make a whole.

What they create instead is an illusion I call the satisfaction trap.

Think of Magellan's sixteenth-century quest for a west-bound passage to the Spice Islands of the East Indies. His navigational instruments were highly inaccurate, and his charts showed vast unexplored—even blank—territories. In spite of those difficulties, his crew did eventually find the Spice Islands. They accomplished what no man had done before: They circumnavigated the globe. But whether they achieved this triumph because of their navigational skill, or despite it, is open to debate.

Too often, measurements of customer satisfaction are like Magellan's instruments. They tell you very little about where you are, and they can't show you where to go.

There are, to be sure, customers who are satisfied but nevertheless keep suppliers on their toes with frequent gripes. But those are rare. More often companies get feedback only from surveys and answers to casually posed questions at the point of sale: "How would you rate your satisfaction with your purchase?" Managers can always find something in those responses that confirms their particular points of view. They can interpret the same customer satisfaction input in completely different ways, just as pundits can read anything they want into preelection polls or survey data. But surveys and focus groups don't analyze customer feedback with precision, and their results are notoriously susceptible to distortion.

One big problem is who participates—and who doesn't. In my experience, anywhere from 15 to 35 percent of your customers won't respond. Period. Many of those who do tell you just what they think you want to hear. If they're unhappy they endure, awaiting the proverbial backbreaking straw. That's when they up and quit the deal. Perhaps it's in their nature not to complain. Perhaps they don't expect their complaints to have any effect. Either way, the company sustains its disastrous belief that its customers are tickled pink.

At other times, the customer responses may be full and fair. The problem is that they are from the wrong sort of customers—the customers a company would rather off-load on its worst rival.

Then there is a problem of semantics: What do customers mean when they check "above average" on a satisfaction questionnaire, particularly when above average has become today's norm? Their above average could mean nothing more than a worldly sigh, or a cynical smile. As any seasoned market researcher knows, satisfaction is a lot trickier to grasp than most managers recognize.

The second assumption that lies beneath the illusion of customer satisfaction is equally as dangerous as the measurement illusion. Many managers persist in the belief that satisfaction, once measured, will point them in profitable directions. It won't. Sound the depths and shoot the stars as often as he did, his measurements never told Magellan where he should go, or how to get there. For that, he needed a detailed map that didn't exist. Likewise, while it seems a noble goal to pursue higher levels of satisfaction or total satisfaction, it's equally devoid of specificity.

Establishing satisfaction as the ultimate goal is like the other ultimate goals of business: pursuit of higher profits or shareholder wealth. They are admirable objectives, but they don't tell managers what to do. They fail to specify priorities and focus. Such objectives don't map the journey ahead—the discovery of better value and solutions for the customer. Give three managers the same objective: To improve customer satisfaction, however it may be measured. Chances are they'll come up with three distinctly different and incompatible plans.

THE PROBLEM OF PARTIAL SOLUTIONS

If you browse through today's bookstores or thumb through recent issues of business magazines, you could easily think that customer satisfaction is the name of a booming new industry, a hotbed of innovation that managers ignore at their peril. There are the secrets of "keeping buyers for life," the latest prescriptions to "customerize" the world, or the discovery of how to "reengineer our relationships."

Our world, unfortunately, is not so simple. All of the newly minted, customer-driven concepts arise from absolutely the best intentions. And managers follow them with the best intentions, too. More often than not, however, they are prescriptions for disappointment, delivering far less than they promise. They are reactive rather than proactive: They address only specific aspects of customers' existing needs rather than projecting new, creative, and remunerative possibilities. And, they are often expensive: They impress the customer at the risk of bankrupting the supplier.

Taken at face value, many of those nostrums present a sound logic and a kinship to the discipline of customer intimacy. But they are all partial solutions, and, as such, they fall short of providing each customer with the best total solution for his or her unique requirements.

Here are five prominent approaches that all aim to boost satisfaction, and as a consequence are likely to disappoint. As the Romans might have put it: caveat venditor—let the seller beware.

Partial Solution One: Consultative Selling

Logic: *Help customers define their problem, and then sell them the best offering.*

Caveat: *It will backfire if it's no more than a great sales pitch without operations backup and solid delivery.*

The notion of consultative selling has been around for decades and enjoys regular revival as the great panacea for all business-development problems. The logic is impeccable: The sales force—usually with titles like account manager or sales consultant—wins customers' respect by listening to them and helping them cope with their specific problems. Of course, customers often need assistance as they deal with increasingly complex products. This is especially true when a product is new, technologically challenging, or is used in combination with other products that create mix-and-match problems.

The aim of consultative selling is to make customers understand precisely what's causing their difficulty, before you sell them anything. That in itself is a laudable tactic that can win the customer's business, but it can also turn into a complete fiasco if the supplier doesn't back up its initial consulting effort with competent solution delivery.

Too often it's a case of great sizzle, bad steak. Successful consultative selling relies on flawless coordination between sales and operations. When those are out of sync, it doesn't matter how exact your promise—you can't deliver.

Partial Solution Two: Service Recovery

Logic: *Customers celebrate suppliers who turn a negative experience—a service mishap—into a positive one.*

Caveat: *If service recovery becomes part of standard operating procedure, it can mask the underlying problems and cause the same mishaps again and again.*

Customers who lavish praise on a supplier's unexpected recovery from a service fumble are not telling the supplier that it's now all right to institutionalize screwups. I remember when my wife's luggage didn't make it to Colorado, the airline did a stellar job of recovering it within a day. It even supplied her with a temporary replacement ski outfit until hers arrived. Nevertheless, she'd never welcome another demonstration of that skill. What she wanted was her own ski suit and, for that, she had to wait.

Such Oops!-But-I'll-Make-It-Wonderful-For-You tales are often cited with admiration. Reportedly, the result is stronger customer loyalty and positive word of mouth. Undoubtedly, it's good to remedy any service failures speedily and competently. Those who goofed get a soft landing, and the company may even earn a good name for quick retrievals.

Although faultless service is more or less invisible and rarely makes for good anecdotes, companies that can provide it don't end up spending endless time, money, and energy cleaning up after their messes. And, instinctively, customers turn to the company that makes the fewest mistakes.

Beware of cheerful superheroes who forget their job exists only because of disasters that should never happen.

Partial Solution Three: Recognition and Loyalty Programs

Logic: *Customers will be more loyal when they receive personal attention that sets them apart from others.*

Caveat: *Don't make friendliness training, knowing customers' names, and occasional freebies a substitute for tangible value.*

Repeat car buyers and regular travelers on the airlines know that respectful treatment and frequent-user bonuses are welcome dividends on top of first-rate value. Most consumers and business customers hanker for personal recognition and signs that they're appreciated. Thus, recognition and loyalty programs can make a difference— particularly when the supplier is in a commodity market where the buyer perceives little distinction between competitors' offerings. A smile and a gift may be enough to keep a customer from wandering to the next shop front.

Recognition and loyalty programs can sweeten a deal and even compensate for certain shortcomings. But they are no substitute for the benefits customers expect from your core offering. Take the example of us business travelers: No amount of frequent-flyer miles will get us to put up with airlines that are infamous for being behind schedule. And don't we prefer a capable but unsmiling cabin crew member to the cheerful chatterbox who mispronounces our name and spills a drink in our lap?

Friendliness, loyalty, and incentive programs do have roles, but their roles have limits. On their own, they become superficial parodies of the personalized results customer intimacy delivers.

Partial Solution Four: Customer Care

Logic: *The more you cozy up, the more likely it is that a win–win relationship can be developed.*

Caveat: *Don't get close to the wrong people, or get too close for comfort.*

When it comes to caring about the customer, more isn't always better. Not only can it blunt objectivity and initiative, it can also overload systems and schedules. It can generate complexities that don't add value. And it can create friction.

Beware of caring so much that you crowd your customers. Some prize their independence, the freedom to go where they want, looking to drive the best bargain in a highly competitive marketplace. Such customers find closeness repellent, and they're unlikely to share their thoughts, needs, or operational plans without an extremely compelling reason.

Customer intimacy gives them that reason. It promises results: better business for supplier and customer alike.

Partial Solution Five: Micromarketing

Logic: *Boost satisfaction by dividing your mass market into tiny segments, giving customized treatment to each.*

Caveat: *Unbridled variety and imprecise targeting can undermine the expected outcome.*

The logic of micromarketing is compelling. By fine-tuning your products and communications programs and addressing the desires of a multitude of microsegments, you can make nearly one-of-a-kind offerings. Not a bad idea, but beware of plunging your customers into the grief of choice overload or pseudopersonalization.

Choice overload occurs when suppliers mistake unbridled product variety for customization. They produce an extensive range of models, types, and sizes in the hope that one will do. The complexity of choices often leaves customers frustrated, irritated, or confused, feeling like diners in a restaurant who have to deal with a 12-page menu written in a language they forgot once they graduated high school. There's no lack of choices, but where's the translation that makes selection possible?

Mere variety and multiple choice make choosing the right solution the customer's job. And that's a job they may not be prepared to handle. Think about buying a personal computer system today. To find the one just for you may mean remembering so many variables that you feel the need for a statistician to run regression analyses. Failing that, you simply take the suggestion of the last person whom you consulted. You might have done better to throw darts. And multiple choice makes customers uneasy. Ask people who have had to choose among different medical insurance plans. They'll tell you that the only answer they really wanted was to a question they couldn't ask: "What are you trying to hide from me here?" Multiple choice is also costly, and customers are clever enough to realize that they are the ones who end up paying for the higher inventory, financing, and handling costs.

Sometimes suppliers flood their microsegments with messages that seem to single out customers for individual consideration. The truth is, however, they treat them like numbers. I call that pseudo-personalization. You know what I mean if complete strangers have ever sent you one of those Dear-Mr.-Brown: You-have-been-selected-for-our-special-offer letters. Pseudopersonalization is the result of imprecise targeting. The supplier who has no specific details on individual customers or prospects resorts to a game of chance: If you live in a certain neighborhood and have bought certain classes of products, you're likely to fit a pattern the supplier has sketched. Sophisticated practitioners go so far as to call their approach precision targeting. The term has a nice ring. Does it surprise you to learn that many of its advocates operate in the direct-marketing field, where response rates for a catalog mailing hover around 2 percent? Some precision.

Micromarketing and the other four partial solutions I've described all share the same shortcomings: They address only part of a customer's problem. Each one stands on the filmy illusion that "customer satisfaction" is attainable. And that, as we have seen, is folly.

It's time to promise customers something more than mere satisfaction. It's time to commit to customer intimacy.

3 | THE COMMITMENT OF INTIMACY

The core of customer intimacy lies in a simple—but radical—commitment: to deliver results. Not satisfaction, not delight, but the best possible solution to an individual customer's needs. Customer-intimate companies can sell virtually anything: plastics, insurance, auto seats, tools, flowers, fitness gear, trucking services, custom-crafted electronic components, or outsourced data management. But whatever they're selling, their commitment to their customers' best results remains the same.

Simple logic lies behind that commitment. Customer-intimate companies know their customers don't buy a product or a service. They buy its benefits. The bigger the benefits, the more product or service they'll buy—a result that pays off for buyer and seller alike.

What's radical about this is the depth of commitment its execution requires. To deliver best results takes all the imagination, initiative, empathy, and dedication a company can muster to stretch its understanding of its mission, its organization, its culture, and its customers.

Listen to how customer-intimate managers sell. Whatever specific benefit they offer a potential customer, they always invoke the same eloquent commitment, which they can express simply and directly enough to pass "the elevator test."

You know what I mean. You get on the elevator and head for a meeting with your prospect on the 27th floor—but when the elevator stops on 3, the prospect walks in, looking harried. He's got to cancel, he says, but he'll be glad to listen to your pitch on the way up to his floor. This gives you maybe 30 seconds to make a distinctive impression—to get your value proposition across.

Customer-intimate managers know what to say. They'll talk results, hard and tangible. No generalizations. No partial solutions. They focus on the individual across from them, not a group or demographic construct. They understand that each customer's needs are unique and present an opportunity to deliver a unique solution. They don't say, "That's too difficult" or "We don't do things that way." Instead they say, "Let's explore what we can do for you."

Promises, when you get right down to it, are the souls of all businesses. But the promising soul of a customer-intimate company is special. Its soul is alive with the knowledge and experience that the customer's results drive its own results; the customer's wins are its wins; the customer's productivity increases are its productivity increases. Those convictions charge commitments with energy. Back in the elevator, your every word carries the electrifying subtext: "You pay us upon performance. Performing for you is all that matters to us."

Of course, your promise must deliver more than electricity. Results promised must be results you will deliver: ambitiously conceived, carefully crafted, and relentlessly improved. That's where customer intimacy gets intricate.

AN OFFER YOU CAN'T REFUSE

How's this for a value proposition? "We'll handle your personnel worries better than you can. And we'll set you free to concentrate on your strengths."

Or this? "We'll give you a no-surprises new-product rollout. And we'll take complete responsibility for design and manufacturing—whenever you ask, whatever you need."

Those are the kinds of promises that grab customers' attention and that push customer-intimate suppliers to industry leadership.

Ceridian Corporation is an information services company whose Ceridian Employer Services business looks for corporate clients with complex payroll, tax, or human resource problems, and solves them comprehensively, one customer at a time. It can, for example, handle all aspects of its customers' payrolls: Ceridian's software—which gives it remote access to the payroll database on any of a customer's personal computers—allows it to prepare the customer's payroll, print the checks, and deliver them to employees on time. Ceridian's total human resource solution packages include its unique employee-assistance program, which helps the workforce solve such puzzles of daily life as eldercare, childcare, financial concerns, and workplace issues.

For the customer, the result is a happier workforce and the freedom to concentrate on a core competency. For Ceridian, the result has been a growing reputation as an industry leader, and, in only three years, sales and profits have grown dramatically.

Johnson Controls didn't simply design a seat for the new Chrysler Neon. The company took responsibility for an entire system, from product planning and styling to design engineering, source control, and assembly. Johnson's engineers worked day by day in partnership with the automaker's engineers to make sure product and process delivered what the market demanded. Johnson took responsibility for coordinating all the subcontractors, and, to ensure just-in-time integrated manufacturing, it built its new plant next door to Chrysler's.

Results for Chrysler? A better seat for a better car, thanks to collaboration.

Results for Johnson Controls? An enviable customer list that includes Ford, General Motors, Chrysler, Toyota, Honda, Nissan, Mercedes, Volkswagen, Rover, and Renault.

What does it take to deliver such mutually rewarding results? How does a company move from the concept and promise of customer intimacy to its practice and profit? How do promises made become promises delivered?

There are three principles to follow—the three imperatives, if you will, of intimacy:

➤ *Number one:* Flex your commercial imagination. Search ambitiously for ever-better solutions to your customers' needs. It's never enough to see the world as your customers do. You have to see it more clearly. Probe their markets and their operations, their habits and their hopes. Imagination stretches your customers' expectations—and your own.

➤ *Number two:* Cultivate your human connections. Intimacy is not a transaction, a one-shot exchange you forget once you book the revenue. It's a dynamic relationship of trust and openness that grows as you deliver results, dependably, time after time. Choose relationships carefully and nourish them to protect their promise of mutually improving productivity.

➤ *Number three:* Commit, commit, commit. Intimacy breaks ground with new demands and new relationships. Meeting those demands and cultivating those relationships—day by day, one customer at a time—takes agility and flexibility, with a culture, systems, measurements, and economics to match.

Those three principles—imagination, connection, and commitment—are intertwined and interdependent. As demanding as each one is, you must pursue those principles simultaneously or you will fail.

FLEX YOUR IMAGINATION

"When a customer tells me I should treat him 'like a king,' I know to watch my wallet," one business executive told me. "He could cost me a fortune."

His point was well taken. Kowtowing to your customers' every wish or guideline guarantees trouble. Partnerships founded on radical inequality just can't last. But that executive had another, more subtle, point to make. It's equally true that most customers don't have the foggiest notion of what the "best result" might be. So the first imperative of intimacy is to exercise your commercial imagination: Find that single best result, and direct your customer to it.

"Direct" doesn't mean that the customer must kowtow to you; it means simply that you must lead the way forward. Understand your customers' needs, their identity, and potential. Take responsibility for their success.

There's truth in the old saw that when customers ask for a drill, what they really want is holes. Delivering the right drills means asking what kind of holes they need.

But that's only your first question. Intimacy demands that you understand the customers' business better than they themselves do. Why do they need holes? What do they hope to accomplish? How do they hope to accomplish it? Do they need help with the drills?

Do their people need training? Do they need help purchasing related equipment and supplies?

Getting answers to such questions, as we shall see in more detail in Part II, is an exercise in initiative and imagination.

I'm not referring to such initiatives as offering a broader range of products or services or imaginative responses to service mishaps. As we have seen, those are reactive activities: They respond to what customers ask for or expect. Flexing commercial imagination is proactive: You must get to the heart of customers' requirements, shape their behavior, and steer them to new, ever richer solutions. It means exploring tomorrow's possibilities rather than yesterday's solutions. There is always a better way. Gather information and apply your understanding: The more solid intelligence you get to nourish your company's creative faculty, the brighter and sharper its inventions. Encourage openness: Information hoarded is information squandered.

How deep will a customer-intimate enterprise probe? As deep as it takes to discover its customers' real needs. For Black & Decker, as we saw in Chapter 1, it meant taking an anthropologist's approach. For Microsoft's Eric LeVine, it meant a month of shuttling from law firm to law firm, watching customers use their word-processing software, keystroke by keystroke. For industrial cutting-tool manufacturer Kennametal, it meant sending 300 employees from its factory to its customer's factory, so they could all see firsthand the job Kennametal's tools had to accomplish.

Customers, unfortunately, often don't know or can't express what they want; more often still they don't know what they need. So customer-intimate suppliers will educate them, define their expectations, and teach them how to get the greatest benefit from their purchases.

Calyx & Corolla, the San Francisco–based mail-order flower company, solves those problems by making it easy to purchase flowers—

by mail, fax, or phone. Furthermore, C&C steps in to help customers select just the right flowers for special occasions and to find new ways to use flowers as part of their everyday decor. Customers know they can consult C&C's "plant doctor" by dialing an 800 number for coaching on how to care for their flowers and plants.

Wisconsin-based Quad/Graphics does much the same for the commercial customers who buy its printing services. Catalog-and-magazine-production (CAMP) customers flock to "CAMP/Quad" for two or three days of fun and instructive seminars on the details of innovative printing. The better its customers understand printing, Quad believes, the better their printing will be.

The mass-market retail customers of Bollinger Industries, a leading distributor and marketer of such exercise accessories as jump ropes, dumbbells, and exercise mats, have come to expect Bollinger's distinctive marketing presentations and displays, customer service and support, inventory management, and cooperative advertising. But those customers—companies like Kmart, Wal-Mart, Oshman's Sporting Goods, and Sears—needed more: They wanted more consumers coming into their stores, and they wanted larger sales per consumer. Bollinger gave them more. It took responsibility for the needs of its customers' customers. For example: Joggers suffer shin splints and weight lifters pull muscles. But the sporting goods aisles stocked no remedies. Bollinger responded by developing more than 40 kinds of sports-medicine and health and safety products.

The results were astonishing. Bollinger's retail customers' stores attracted more shoppers whose individual tabs were larger than ever before. Bollinger's new products contributed handsomely to its top line. And consumers were happier, too: They took Bollinger sports accessories to the gym, and when aches and pains overcame them, they treated themselves with other Bollinger products.

CULTIVATE YOUR CONNECTIONS

Too many business managers think traditionally when it comes to company-to-company relationships. They think "compete," or they think "merge and acquire." Anything in between is discomforting, if not unintelligible. They, therefore, keep their suppliers at arm's length, pitting vendor against vendor in search of the temporary advantage. They don't allow themselves to discover what cooperation could do for all of them.

Intimacy, however, demands the better way. Intimacy demands connection, a working relationship grounded in trust and built over time. The daily give and take between customer and supplier, searching together for mutually beneficial results, form the foundation of genuine intimacy.

Trust doesn't develop on its own. It takes honesty and openness, an eagerness to understand one another's strengths and weaknesses, and willingness to share information and intelligence. And trust doesn't develop overnight. Supplier and customer alike must believe that each is upholding its end of the deal. They must define expectations clearly, explicitly, and mutually. And both must meet those expectations. Call it the no-surprises imperative: the confidence that the other side will come through, time and time again.

You must custom-craft each connection, like every best result, based on the free exchange of specific intelligence concerning needs, attitudes, habits, and behaviors. But not every prospect has the potential for intimacy. You must choose your customers and your connections carefully. Are they open to collaboration, or are they caught in the traditional web of suspicion? Do their values—and their economics—fit yours? Many customer-intimate companies look for "stretch" customers—customers whose needs test their abilities and, as a result, promise the greatest potential for dramatic results.

Launching a relationship is hard work. Making it work is harder still. How can you instill confidence? Can your solution expand to cover other aspects of your customer's needs? Are there ways to improve communications? Can you assume greater responsibility for your customer's results? You must cultivate and enrich every customer connection. Discard the old styles of communication and mistrust. Destroy the us-versus-them barriers and distinctions between supplier and customer.

For Ohio-based Caliber Logistics, Inc., formerly known as Roadway Logistics Systems (ROLS), it means tackling a customer's toughest problem. By 1991, the shipping department of Libbey-Owens-Ford (LOF), one of the nation's largest producers of automotive-safety and architectural glass, was in chaos: too many vendors, too many unnecessary expenses, and administrative costs that were way too high. There was neither a central database available to track its purchases nor a way to leverage its volume.

ROLS viewed the LOF situation as a challenge. It shouldered the task of simplifying and streamlining the connections between LOF's 12,000 vendors and its 105 plants. It designed efficient inbound and outbound tracking systems and replaced the annual deluge of 83,000 freight bills with 52 electronic transmissions—one each week.

Results? In the first year alone, ROLS cut LOF's total logistics costs by more than $800,000.

But Caliber Logistics knows that it must continue to nourish the LOF connection. To keep their connection flourishing, the two companies must continue to work together to uncover sources of savings. Some companies strengthen productive ties with their customers by broadening their connections. They parlay their customer's hard-won confidence into searches for new ways to further productivity.

Most innovative customer connections illustrate an interesting transition. As suppliers and customers learn to work together, building confidence as they grow, the lines of distinction between them grow blurry, as if the two were different aspects of a single organization, jointly pursuing mutual success.

Look, for example, at the relationship between Marshall Industries, the giant electronics distributor, and contract manufacturer Diagnostic Instrument, one of Marshall's larger accounts. An outsider would be hard-pressed to tell where one company ends and the other begins. The two companies sell together. They forecast together. They've abolished separate purchase orders, bills, invoices, and accounting. They use software that links the two of them, allowing them to run their consigned material system jointly. The Marshall's account rep even sits in on Diagnostic's purchasing meetings. "We kid him all the time that we're going to give him a Diagnostic Instrument time card," Diagnostic's CEO James Hashem says. "We've already given him a desk, a chair, and a telephone, and he's on our E-mail as well as Marshall's. It certainly cuts communication time, and time is money for both of us."

COMMIT, COMMIT, COMMIT

By now it should be clear to you that customer intimacy is not a discipline for the faint of heart. It's less traditional than operational excellence or product leadership. It's more relationship driven, and it focuses uniquely on mutual results with each customer. Conventional-minded managers may find the customer-intimate approach alien—a strange land with radical assumptions and a barely understandable language.

Consider the words a customer-intimate manager might use to describe his ideal prospect:

complex
variable
taxing
fuzzy

Intimacy thrives, intellectually and financially, on difficulty. A good prospect is one that is engaged in (and perhaps overwhelmed by) complex operations. Its needs, insofar as it can describe them, will be fuzzy. Those needs vary continually, changing in sudden and unpredictable ways.

As a result, the customer-intimate company must cultivate some outstanding characteristics of its own:

agility
judiciousness
diplomacy
foresight
willingness

What do I mean when I say that the "company" must cultivate those characteristics? I mean, simply, that the executives must take care to ensure that everyone values those qualities of mind and heart: not just leaders, salespeople, field operators, and the like, but everyone in the company. The distinctiveness of customer intimacy is, perhaps above all, a cultural distinctiveness.

From top to bottom—or, more likely, from center to periphery—customer-intimate companies must foster agility that lets them respond to their customers' individual variability and foresight to minimize their customers' unpredictability. The customer-intimate company must have judiciousness to see through their customers' fuzziness, and diplomatic skills to effect the old adage, "Always try to let the other guy have your way." Willingness, of course, is the heart of the customer-intimate culture: a constant disposition to serve the customer.

Obviously, such a culture engenders organizational consequences. Companies that follow that discipline are not likely to respond to traditional, hierarchical, top-down management, nor are they likely to survive a highly centralized structure. You can't create connections with your customers, nor can you manage their needs, from the "top" or from the "center." Decision-making at the local level, on the other hand, can deal with each client situation and demand on the spot.

The best way to maintain your equilibrium in a customer-intimate practice is by making sure that throughout your organization everyone feels the close collaboration you establish with your customer in the field, as if there were a shared corporate nervous system. Frontline and back-office employees have to orchestrate a rapport between, say, what the sales department promises and what the factory can deliver. Most customer-intimate companies invest heavily in communications and information technology. Such systems must, of course, be flexible enough to serve multiple requirements: to capture customer intelligence, to create communication links, to deliver solutions.

For Samsung Electronics, the journey to intimacy starts when the telephone rings. For years, when Samsung's customers called with questions they were shunted from department to department. Finally, in response to mounting frustration, the electronics manufacturer assembled a brainstorming team from various departments, talked to customers about how to improve, and—using an integrated software system that put all the company's departments on-line, with real-time accessibility—redesigned the connection.

Their solution, the Business Operations Center, allows customers to dial a well-publicized phone number for easy access to hard information about product specifications, pricing, order entry, invoicing, shipping, and billing. It is not yet intimacy, admits manager Richard Choi, but "We do not want them to have to waste time on us in order to find the correct information." But it is a start—and a spur to Samsung's ambition. By the year 2000, Choi says, the company should be able "to answer any kind of question that a customer presents within two minutes—and deliver within two days."

What processes will a customer-intimate company redesign? Any that are necessary to deliver results. Calyx & Corolla, the flower company, developed both a new supply and a new delivery system, affecting not only its own operations but the operations and practices of their most important vendors as well.

C&C's commitment to delivering only the freshest flowers created logistical challenges at both ends of the system. Unlike its competitors who use local florists to fill orders, C&C eliminated middlemen, whose slow route to delivery often took 5 to 10 days. C&C recognized, however, that the local florists did play a vital role in each transaction: They packaged the orders. To make its system work, C&C persuaded their growers not simply to ship in bulk but also to assemble and pack individual bouquets. Next, C&C convinced its air carrier, Federal Express, to work with them: FedEx would pick up directly from the independent growers, rather than funneling their orders through a central warehouse. The shipper already made Saturday deliveries: This was essential. After all, many of the occasions that call for flowers—weddings, birthdays, Mother's Day, and so forth—take place on weekends. What's more, C&C had to persuade FedEx to leave packages at unanswered doors. C&C would assume liability.

Scania, the Swedish automotive manufacturer, enjoys an enviable record: It has recorded profits in every quarter for the past 60 years. Scania consistently outperforms such competitors as Volvo and Mercedes—matching or exceeding their quality, operating at a lower cost, and earning an enviable 80 percent customer retention rate.

The key to Scania's enduring success lies in its ability to tailor each truck or bus to match customer specifications—specifications that derive from variations in climate, terrain, and road quality.

It takes agility to build vehicles one at a time. Modular manufacturing gives customers choices: any combination of 10 different engine sizes; low- or high-elevation cab; four, six, or eight wheels, and so on. Modularity cuts costs. To provide the same range of choice, Mercedes must stock 40,000 truck components. Scania stocks 20,000 and passes its savings on to customers. But modular manufacturing wouldn't work without a modular management structure. Local operating units have the autonomy and authority to make decisions and explore innovative, comprehensive solutions—one customer at a time. Scania calls its process coordinated independence. By spreading authority throughout its organization, the company has flattened its hierarchy. The corporate planning staff now totals a sparse 20 people.

Such agility frees the commercial imagination. It builds productive connections that inspire unequaled customer loyalty.

PART II

Flex the Commercial Imagination

Why would customers throw open their doors to suppliers, embrace them warmly, and treat them like dear friends-or close relatives? Why would they let them poke around in their bureau drawers and medicine cabinets, talk openly with every member of the family, and help themselves to the contents of the refrigerator? What exactly do customer-intimate companies bring to the party that makes them such treasured and trusted guests?

The answer is simple: Customer-intimate businesses come promising better results. Not bits and pieces that might contribute to a happy outcome, but the outcome itself. Not "Here's what I'm trying to sell you," but "Here's how much better your life will be when we're up and running."

Only by promising total solutions can a customer-intimate company establish strong, durable bonds with a customer. And, considering what we know about today's sophisticated and demanding customers, the promise itself had better be outstanding: credible, concise, and compelling. But to make a solid, succinct promise, you must have a workable, total solution. To have a solution, you must know the problem. To know the problem, you must know the customer. And to keep all those balls in the air, you must know your own strengths and weaknesses.

There's no shortcut to such insight and understanding. You must exert all your muscle and brain power and tap into every resource available. And you still have more to do. Customer intimacy requires companies to look at the world through the customers' eyes and see it better than they do. This demands logic, inspiration, intellect, and inventiveness—in short, imagination.

This section of the book deals with the ways in which customer-intimate firms stimulate the imagination and apply their creative thinking. In Chapter 4 we'll focus on using commercial imagination to probe the depths of customers' real problem—beyond the immediate needs to recognize themselves. In Chapters 5, 6, and 7, we'll discuss how following one of the three most fruitful paths to intimacy can turn understanding of a problem into the best total solution.

4 | WHAT'S THE REAL PROBLEM?

If I were to pick the single most important question a customer-intimate company can ask about its customer, it would have to be: What's the real problem here? Not the troublesome symptoms, not the complicating circumstances. What is the basis, the actuality, the root of it all? Before a company can fulfill the first commitment of intimacy—to direct its customer to a total solution—it must answer that central question.

Most customers, unfortunately, can't describe their real problems; often they don't know themselves. Real problems are hard to spot, especially for managers so involved in day-to-day operations that they have inadequate perspective to see the big picture. But outsiders can bring a fresh eye and a different state of mind. Outsiders spot opportunities where the customer sees only trouble. Outsiders can look deeply enough and far enough into the future to see how trouble can be turned into triumph.

They can—and they must. As Chris Peters, vice president of the Microsoft Office product unit, points out, "If you give people only what they say they want, they'll probably go out of business in five years. And so will you. You have to read between the lines and listen to the silences before you start responding."

Listening to the silences—those needs customers can't articulate and may not know they have—is the only way to answer the question, "What's the real problem here?" Intimacy demands understanding how your customer perceives the value of a purchase—in a broad context that includes the cycle of buying, using, fixing, and replacing it. Intimacy demands pushing beyond a customer's surface problem to its root cause. You must explore the customer's hierarchy of needs: the problem behind the problem behind the problem. And intimacy demands predicting how today's problems and opportunities might change tomorrow. You must practice the art of anticipation.

Let's look at each of the three demands you must meet to create true customer intimacy.

THE CUSTOMER'S EXPERIENCE CYCLE

Remember your last visit to a restaurant with fine food and frustratingly bad service? If you had to wait an hour for your appetizer, you undoubtedly valued the chef's culinary skills a lot lower than you would have if the food had arrived after a 15-minute wait. Dining, after all, is more than food on the plate. It's a total evening's experience.

That's true for every purchase of a service or product. Whether they buy retail or business-to-business, customers base the perceived value of their purchases on more than the specifications, features, and price. Their impressions during the cycle of acquiring, owning, and ultimately discarding the product—what I call the customer's Get-It, Use-It, and Fix-It experiences—also contribute to the customer's perceptions of value. By understanding each customer's experience through an entire cycle, a supplier can cast a larger net around the customer's real needs.

Get-It is part of the acquisition process: from searching for and choosing the product and supplier, through ordering, shipment, delivery, installation, and payment. Each step makes an impression—rational and emotional, positive or negative—that either enhances or diminishes perceived value. Setting up meetings with company sales reps, booking rental car reservations, reading advertisements and promotional material—all are aspects of the Get-It package.

Use-It stretches over time, through a customer's experiences of product performance. Was it easy to get started? Was the manual clear? How did the product hold up? Did it do the job readily and as well as it should have? Use-It satisfaction grows consistently as the product's performance meets the expectations raised by promises in contracts, catalogs, and advertisements.

Fix-It comes at the end of the cycle, when products need attention and mending. Everything that interrupts product use—regular maintenance, upgrades, repairs after the inevitable, occasional breakdown—creates another customer impression. Positive or negative, such impressions take on particular importance when the time comes to look for a new model and start the cycle again.

A customer buys a product, but he or she wants to get an entire set of satisfying experiences. Therefore, the supplier's goal must be to improve the entire spectrum of Get-It, Use-It, Fix-It: to make acquiring products and services more pleasant, ensure they're properly used, and facilitate quick and effective repairs and adjustments. The tricky part is that one customer's experiences seldom match those of another: people perceive, interpret, and appreciate differently. Customer-intimate suppliers understand those differences and shape the experiences in ways their selected customers most appreciate.

Barnes & Noble bookstores, for example, are polishing up the Get-It experience by redesigning their interiors. B&N is adding comfortable seats, coffee bars, appealing music, and a host of other atmosphere enhancers. The bookseller is transforming the process of browsing and selecting books into an experience that is a pleasant, Get-It treat.

Saturn, a subsidiary of General Motors, began with the Get-It experience, its novel no-haggling policy addressing consumers' common dislike of negotiating with car salesmen. This is an example of Saturn working hard to generate customer enthusiasm for both the product and the company. Saturn also worked closely with its retailers as partners to enable this type of intimacy to become a part of its culture. But Saturn also looked at Use-It and Fix-It and built customer loyalty with such innovative offerings as free towing and car rental following breakdowns, and complimentary hotel rooms when a mechanical malfunction forces an owner to spend a night on the road while his or her car is being serviced.

British Airways (BA), on the other hand, began by addressing the Fix-It experiences. BA knew that tales of bad experiences spread faster than do praises. It therefore redesigned the company's responses to such service mishaps as lost luggage, canceled flights, and overbooking. Then BA addressed the Get-It and Use-It aspect of the cycle. It introduced a company-wide policy of seamless service to improve every detail of BA passengers' experiences. BA retrained its reservation specialists. It improved airport-counter service to reduce waiting time. It refurbished its airport lounges with such amenities as complimentary phone service, television monitors, and a wide assortment of magazines and newspapers for its business travelers. Results? In the decade since it initiated its overhaul, BA's annual revenues have doubled.

Customer-intimate companies that market to other companies, rather than to end-user consumers, face a steeper challenge. It's increasingly difficult for suppliers to compete on their Get-It strengths, since defect-free purchasing in the commercial arena has become commonplace. And with product quality and reliability up, a similar situation exists for Fix-It experiences. The growing focus is on heightening the Use-It benefits. Such high-tech companies as Hewlett-Packard and NCR Corporation, for example, send out highly educated and well-trained sales forces to identify their customers' requirements. They can then offer them individualized systems solutions. GE Plastics, as we have seen, does much the same with its productivity teams.

No matter where a supplier decides to compete, however, the customer's perception of value is directly related to his or her experiences through the Get-It, Use-It, Fix-It cycle. Unless all three experiences are positive, the supplier has not met the full range of the customer's needs.

THE HIERARCHY OF CUSTOMER NEEDS

When you explore a customers' experience cycle, you can learn exactly what is valued in a purchase—that is, the whole package, the entire context of that purchase. The next essential step is understanding why the customer wants that package. Move your imaginative thinking from the what to the why.

That calls for you to answer harder questions, but it takes you closer to the real problem. Once again you can't expect the customer to be able to articulate the answer. A customer sees only surface problems. You have to see beyond those urgent, self-reported desires to the customer's more entrenched, long-term, perhaps even unrecognized needs, climbing up what the American psychiatrist Abraham Maslow called, in another context, a hierarchy of needs.

Let's look at the hierarchy of needs in a customer's context. At the most basic level, a customer may think he needs a product or service you can provide. But what he really needs is a result—a hole drilled, if you will—and the drill might not provide the best way to make that hole. Or the customer may not need a new hole after all. Perhaps he needs to improve his usage process or create a completely new process.

For Libbey-Owens-Ford (LOF), the automotive and architectural glass company we saw in Chapter 3, the surface problem seemed to be package delivery. LOF was drowning in deliveries, invoices, delays, and cost overruns. So it turned to Roadway Logistics Systems (ROLS), now Caliber Logistics, Inc., for delivery. But ROLS recognized that LOF's real problem lay farther up its hierarchy of needs. LOF didn't need a new carrier. It already juggled dozens of vendors. It didn't even need a better carrier. It needed an entirely new shipping system—a completely reengineered process.

Working your way up a customer's hierarchy of needs is delicate work. It takes confidence and courage, as well as imagination and tact, to push forward, relentlessly asking why and what for. Slowly, carefully, the questions mount: "What is this product for?" becomes "What is that process for?" which escalates into the old zinger "What business are you in, anyway?" It's a rare company that actively encourages the customer to question everything from its processes to its procedures to its founding principles.

Let me give you an example from my personal experience. Not long ago, one of my consulting clients, a leading European retailer, wanted help in its overhaul of the company's procurement process.

When I met with the retailer's executives, I first wanted to understand the context in which they viewed their problem. I asked how the current procurement process compared with those of the company's competitors. Almost unanimously, the executives agreed that their process was far and away the industry's best. Next, I asked about in-store service. Their response was far less enthusiastic. Most of the executives ranked their service number three industry-wide. Some even considered that ranking optimistic.

Slightly puzzled, I asked why they wanted to reengineer a procurement process that was in relatively good shape rather than the in-store service process that they knew was flawed. The procurement process, they explained, had the most potential, and besides, they'd tried everything they could think of to improve customer service and had pretty much given up.

Unwilling to accept that as the final word, I continued to probe. How good was the company's demand management, a third core process? How effectively did advertising and promotions attract customers into the store? Did merchandise appear on the shelves at the best moments for the right prices? Did they time their sales correctly?

At my first mention of demand management, the room split into hostile camps. One camp comprised advertising and marketing people. They were convinced that they were unequaled in their fields and that nobody could do their job better than they. The store people, they maintained, especially the managers, had to get their act together. Clustered on the other side of the room, the managers of store operations presented their decidedly different view. They absolved themselves of guilt and accused the marketing and advertising people of building customer expectations to levels the store could never fulfill.

In short, the opposing camps had totally different views of how well they were doing in demand management. By extension, their take on the real problem differed just as completely. Their disagreement, and their unwillingness to resolve it, had a long history. The executives had asked me to deal with the procurement process because it was the only one that everyone in the room could agree upon.

But I learned from their discussion that the real problem was the conflicting views about the company's priorities: How should they be pursued, and what roles should the various processes play? So I set to focusing everyone on what mattered most: aligning their priorities. With that fixed, their understanding of how to improve operations became clearer. If I hadn't prodded them to climb their hierarchy of needs, we might well have undertaken unrewarding efforts.

THE ART OF ANTICIPATION

Picture a repair van coursing through the streets of a small Midwestern city. The van pulls up in front of the city's tallest building. Two men leap out and dash to the building's management office. "We've come to fix the elevator," they announce. The confused manager explains that the elevator is working perfectly. "Maybe you have the wrong address," says the manager. "We haven't had any problems at all." The repairman replies, "Not yet, but believe me, if we don't adjust the motor, you'll have a lot of riders stranded before lunch hour."

Science fiction? Not at all. In 1984, Otis began installation of REM (Remote Elevator Monitoring), an electronic device that monitors the operating condition of their elevators. The device beams status reports on each elevator to a local center where service personnel await dispatch. The monitors alert dispatchers to malfunctions and even anticipate problems that trigger preventive maintenance. NovaCare, America's largest contract supplier of therapy and rehabilitative services, introduced a patient-monitoring system that tracks patients throughout their hospital stay.

NovaCare and Otis both practice the first half of the art of anticipation: pattern recognition. They look for tomorrow's problem and solve it today. For USAA, the superb San Antonio–based insurance and financial-services company, pattern recognition is an act of corporate memory. The company develops a long-term relationship with its customers. It keeps track of births, deaths, divorces, and marriages, events that inevitably have an impact on customers' future needs. Noting, for example, that a customer's first child is about to enter driver's education, USAA will approach the parent with an aggressive safe-driving plan. When a customer retires, USAA will offer appropriate financial services.

No customer operates in a vacuum, of course. It's not enough to recognize the patterns of the past and project them into the future. The second half of the art of anticipation calls for watching trends: active monitoring of significant events in a customer's competitive environment, pertinent changes in technology, new demands among end consumers, or even changing weather patterns that will affect regional sales and demand. By following and reading market shifts and outside pattern variations that affect their customers, suppliers can anticipate new or changing problems and prepare new and better solutions to them.

Look, for example, at how Johnson Controls, the seat manufacturer we saw in Chapter 3, responded to changes in the auto industry. As consumers demanded ever higher levels of value, companies like Chrysler found that it was no longer efficient or cost-effective to create cars in a single, massive, vertically integrated system. Carmakers needed help from vendors that would take responsibility for major components, making them better, faster, and cheaper. Having anticipated the change, Johnson Controls was ready to deliver, and it worked with Chrysler to create both product and process for the new Neon that delivered the form, fit, and function the market demanded.

FROM REAL PROBLEM TO REAL SOLUTION

Customer intimacy is mix-it-up, dirty-hands work. Passive observation is worthless. Sympathy for a customer's situation is essential, but it's insufficient without a thorough understanding of the buyer's nuts, bolts, brain waves, and business practices. "You have to understand everything the customer does," insists Microsoft's Chris Peters, "at a micro-level of detail."

Some companies, recognizing that many people are uncomfortable with face-to-face interviews, try to work their way up the needs hierarchy with extensive questionnaires and surveys. Others have introduced on-line aids that enable users to sound off and send suggestions, such as Microsoft Wish. But the most effective strategy, as we suggested in *The Discipline of Market Leaders,* is to live in the field, spending a day, a week, or more immersed in the customers' lives. Your imagination is likely to be most relevant when enlivened by the vivid details you glean from smelling, touching, and tasting the elements in your customer's environment.

Don't rely solely on research firms. While there's nothing inherently wrong with using a market research team or hiring an intermediary to find information, customer intimacy depends at least as much on snapshots of the customer's face and desk as on an aerial view of his or her land.

Don't think of your visits as social calls. For its contextual inquiries, as Microsoft calls its observation of customers while they work, the company recently hired experts to teach anthropological techniques. Now Microsoft can diagram the data it gathers in its office visits. Researchers gather artifacts, the documents customers produce, and observations, which include such seemingly odd details as a blank wall calendar, to analyze them.

And don't send just your salespeople. The wider the range of employees who focus on understanding a customer's solutions, the more successful you are likely to be.

Finding the customers' real problem—understanding their Get-It, Use-It, and Fix-It experiences, climbing their hierarchy of needs, and anticipating how those needs might change—is hard work. And it's only a first step. The next, and harder, task is creating a solution, directing the customer to the best possible result.

Although, as we have seen, there are as many best solutions as there are customer problems, there are just three common paths to intimacy, three different models, if you will. Each model—Tailoring, Coaching, or Partnering—aims to develop a different relationship with the customer—and each is simple enough to explain in an elevator statement. Tailoring's commitment is "We'll deliver a made-to-measure solution for your problems." Coaching's is "We'll help you get better results by drilling, instilling, and instructing." Partnering's maxim is "We'll get you where you need to go by traveling together as allies and companions."

Chapters 5, 6, and 7 will examine those three approaches, one by one. But each begins with the same question: What's the real problem here?

5 | THE TAILORING ROUTE: DELIVERING FITTING SOLUTIONS

➤ You're a young Japanese businessman who wants to build a new house. You've got two kids, an in-law who lives with you three months of the year, and a craving for a Jacuzzi in the master bath. None of the prefab homes you've seen meets your requirements, but hiring an architect is beyond your budget. Now what?

Your best bet is to head to Sumitomo Forestry. This ingenious Japanese builder has incorporated the benefits of customization into mass-produced houses. You and a Sumitomo salesperson sit in front of a terminal of the company's CAD/CAM system, and together you construct your dream house on screen: The system allows you to configure quite freely, and the two of you design the layout, rooftop, and assorted amenities from among the seemingly limitless options in the computer's data bank. When you're done, the system prints out a complete list of the materials you'll need and totals your costs.

At the same time, the computer generates an order form and assigns your project to a construction team that will quickly make your design a reality. You get exactly the house you want, and you pay significantly less than you would had you engaged a traditional contractor. And to top it all off, you can move in twice as fast.

➤ You're a prominent clothing manufacturer, purveyor of the most popular line of trousers the world has ever seen. Now, however, you're trying to create a new look that will rivet the attention of consumers. If it's been done before—in any form—you're not interested in doing it.

Faced with such a challenge, Levi Strauss & Company turned to High Point Chemical, a North Carolina–based manufacturer of fabric and garment processing and finishing agents. Instead of offering a choice of ready-made options, High Point's engineers sat down with Levi Strauss & Co.'s designers, managers, and marketers. Together, High Point and Levi Strauss & Co. came up with a vision for a new look, and High Point proceeded to design a system that would make their idea a product. The result? A stonewashed look to the denim—a fashion trend that at one time dominated American casual wear.

➤ You're the administrator of a frantically busy urban hospital. Gauze, scalpels, hypodermic needles, rubber gloves, and thousands of other supplies are nearly as critical to saving lives as are the surgeons themselves. But supply inventories are undependable. Costs are up. Efficiency is down. Patient care suffers. Communication lines that connect the medical staff, the purchasing department, and the suppliers are hopelessly tangled.

The 300-bed Seton Medical Center in Daly City, California, saved $300,000 in 1994, and more than $90,000 in 1995, utilizing the PBDS program. PBDS is an inventory control program based on the number of patient procedures scheduled in a given area, say, cardiology. If 10 procedures are scheduled, 10 modules are ordered. In each kit is a prescribed set of materials with specified amounts needed for the procedure. Everything is premeasured and assembled, so there is no preparatory manpower required and little waste results. There is also no superfluous inventory in storage.

PRODUCE A PERFECT FIT

Tailored solutions are overtaking the marketplace. More and more people are turning to Sumitomo to build them homes in Japan; High Point's profits continue to multiply; Baxter's facility and materials management programs continue to benefit large and small hospitals alike. How? Unlike their competitors, they create, cut, and convert their goods and services to fit each customer's specific needs. Instead of tailoring solutions, other companies are busy doing the opposite: They offer Procrustean beds, not tailored solutions. They stretch or chop their customers' needs to fit their ready-made solutions. Sumitomo's affordable, customized houses, High Point's individually designed finishing agents, and Baxter's inventory control program exemplify a customer-intimate promise: We'll do everything we can to find and deliver the exact product or service that meets your requirements.

Despite the similarity of their approaches those companies illustrate three distinctly different models of tailoring.

Sumitomo gives its customers exactly what they need—as easily and cheaply as possible—by guiding them through an extensive variety of options. Its customers select from an à la carte menu with thousands of dishes.

Together, High Point and its customers evaluate requirements to arrive at a uniquely appropriate solution. Forget the à la carte menu. High Point's customers deal with a personal chef who analyzes their nutritional needs and cooks the meal that's right for them.

Baxter steps in and takes charge of the whole problematic process. It delivers an integrated solution, supplying when it can, outsourcing when it must.

As we examine each of these three models, keep in mind that no one of them is intrinsically more valuable than the others. What matters most is finding the style of tailoring that falls within your capabilities and will serve your customers' needs.

PROVIDE THE RIGHT PRODUCT AT THE RIGHT TIME: THE FIRST MODEL OF TAILORING

Wal-Mart, Price/Costco, and Toys "R" Us deserve the applause they get for their superefficient inventory management, but AutoZone is, in many ways, in its own class. It makes product selection, not selectivity, a virtue. AutoZone offers diagnostic tests, parts, and repair advice to do-it-yourself car owners—it's a sort of vehicular version of Home Depot, the building-supplies chain. Rated by many industry observers as the nation's top retail growth company, AutoZone combines remarkable financial results—over the past five years, sales have tripled and profits increased threefold—with unmatched eagerness to serve its customers well.

The mechanical know-how (or don't-know-how) of the general population is so unpredictable and there is such an extensive assortment of automobile makes and models, that the idea of a personalized, do-it-yourself auto-repair service may seem ludicrous. AutoZone, however, has found a way to give every customer exactly what he or she needs.

Every AutoZone store carries a selection of parts that matches the vehicles that dominate the market in its location. More pickup truck parts in Cheyenne, Wyoming, than in, say, Cincinnati. Furthermore, unless a customer objects, the company stores an electronic record of his or her automotive problems and purchases. Warranty claims are never difficult to confirm—even if a customer has no receipt. Any AutoZone employee (or AutoZoner, as they call themselves) at any of the company's 1,200 outlets has instant access to each customer's purchase and repair history.

AutoZone bases its value proposition on its parts and products inventories, which match a huge variety of needs, and on its individually tailored service. When customers ask for help with oil changes, AutoZone offers them everything they might need to do the job, from oil and filters to drop cloths and extra-strength soap. AutoZone hires people who display enthusiasm for the can-do credo that drives the company.

The AutoZone model of tailoring incorporates a prodigious selection of easily bundled automotive supplies and saves its customers from fruitless trips to more than one auto-supply store. The customers get exactly what—and everything—they need at a great price.

Zeppelin, the primary German distributor of Caterpillar roadworking equipment, uses a similar model of inventory tailoring to produce remarkable results for its customers.

That distributor maximizes the efficiency of its customers' construction and repair operations by minimizing disruptive breakdowns and mechanical failures. Zeppelin promptly responds to emergencies, and does all it can to avoid them altogether. The company is an expert at the art of anticipation: It recommends preventive maintenance, and proposes upgrades and replacements before there's trouble.

It's a big job. Zeppelin handles some 100,000 parts for more than 6,000 customers. Its accounts are scattered throughout Germany—often the customers' road crews work in remote, hard-to-reach places. Should even a small piece of equipment fail, the entire crew can find itself immobilized for days at a cost of tens of thousands of deutsche marks.

Zeppelin masters its enormous inventories by doing away with a one-size-fits-all approach and tailoring its service to each of its customers. The concomitant benefit of Zeppelin's well-tailored service is its extremely lean and effective operation.

Over the years, Zeppelin has built a detailed database of the Caterpillar machines its customers—mostly small- and medium-sized contractors—use, along with their repair records, replacement orders, and usage patterns. That personalized information allows the company to anticipate customers' maintenance and new-equipment needs. Moreover, every time a customer orders a new part, those electronic profiles permit Zeppelin to match the order against the type of machine the customer operates. The sales staff questions any incompatibilities before shipping an order. Recognizing the importance of knowing all its customers' equipment, Zeppelin's sales force gathers information about purchases of its competitors' equipment. Zeppelin is always ready to offer service, and, when appropriate, recommend a switch to a Caterpillar replacement.

Outcome? Zeppelin's central parts distribution system handles three times the volume it did 20 years ago—with the same number of employees. It delivers 98 percent of its orders within 24 hours.

Zeppelin might sum up its value proposition this way: We deliver the right part or machine, at precisely the right moment, at the right price. Because both AutoZone and Zeppelin meet their customers' needs with such precision, it seems as if they fill orders from an unlimited variety of options. In fact, both companies know their customers so well—and have so carefully aligned their businesses to their customers' specific needs—that they have actually reduced their inventories and payrolls, while significantly improving service.

How far should you go to tailor? In addition to well-trained service staffs, companies like Zeppelin and AutoZone use a variety of technological tools that extend their reach into the next century. AutoZone's satellite system allows them to automatically route phone inquiries to call centers in Memphis and Houston. This saves store personnel from constant telephone interruptions, and customers are happy to have their questions answered quickly and efficiently. AutoZone's computer systems help diagnose mechanical failures and identify the parts for repairs. Zeppelin's use of its rich database saves customers time and money, and by preventing emergencies, it frees its own employees from frantic customers' calls from remote locations.

Obviously, not every company manages inventories of an AutoZone or Zeppelin scale. There are alternative tailoring tactics. One is virtual sourcing, as when a car dealer assures a customer that, although the red hatchback with the turbo isn't available on his lot, he can get one delivered—prepped and washed—the very next day. That promise relies on the dealer's computer, which immediately locates the desired model at a nearby dealership.

Since most customers don't care where an item is coming from as long as it arrives when they want it, virtual inventories are increasingly common. Customer-intimate companies establish provider-locator networks that give them access to other companies' offerings, thereby broadening customer choices and lightening inventory loads. Provided you've got the skills to forge such relationships, there's no reason that your à la carte menu can't grow longer and longer, with no sacrifice in quality.

Personalize Your Service

Cable & Wireless Communications (CWI), the United States' leading long-distance carrier exclusively serving businesses, offers a valuable example of how service companies can tailor effectively. CWI conducted a major strategic study in 1993 that revealed that, while it would be difficult to compete with AT&T, MCI, and Sprint on price, it could grow its share of the market by giving customers the kind of options and attention the others couldn't match. CWI took those results to heart and continued to focus its operation on providing a full range of highly customized, feature-rich, telecommunications services, mostly to niche markets of small and midsized companies.

To start, CWI empowered its 48 U.S. sales offices to operate as separate companies. More than mere semantics, that identity encourages each office to look for solutions tailored to the problems of its own customers. As separate companies the offices are more likely to take regional particulars into account. Separate companies took a high level of responsibility for their own customers. Late in 1994, CWI refined the services it extends to industries such as law, engineering, and bookkeeping by introducing software that targets the special needs of each. For example, software for the legal profession, which lets a lawyer track and bill a client's calls, is not altogether adaptable to the needs of engineers. CWI's personalized approach also includes customized billing across the board, security codes and regional calling plans, sales contacts with a real person rather than a mechanized voice, and customer service representatives who troubleshoot and suggest equipment or services changes for maximum savings.

"The long-distance market is less and less about price and more about service," says Gabriel Battista, president and chief executive officer of Cable & Wireless' U.S. operations. Battista is convinced that only segmentation and complete customer responsiveness will triumph in the telecommunications industry free-for-all. While the big three bombard the public with increasingly abrasive, aggressive, and combative ad campaigns and engage in price wars that many consumers find more baffling than beneficial, CWI heeds the quieter and more productive call of tailoring. "We had a simple goal," Battista says. "Find the right customers, learn what they want, sell it to them, and service them in all their needs."

Battista believes CWI's approach works because its business customers (it provides no residential service) value the information CWI's technology provides. It enhances their ability to manage their operations, even though "they don't want to be in the telecommunications business themselves." CWI's tailoring has achieved noteworthy results: Revenues leapt from $365 million in 1991 to $672 million in 1995.

You don't have to be as big as Cable & Wireless to tailor your service. Value Call International of Jacksonville, Florida, by comparison quite small, has found a way to meet its customers' exact needs through veritable tailoring and virtual sourcing. Value Call brokers an extensive list of long-distance networks that includes Cable & Wireless. Those networks offer the best service features and prices for their customers. Let's say Value Call is working with a law firm. If one network has the right long distance service for the firm, and a second network can provide exactly the call-tracking system the firm needs, Value Call will package the two as a seamless service with one simple bill.

Here's how John Honis, one of Value Call's founders, describes his company: "We try to get inside our customers' heads, figure out what they do for a living on a day-to-day basis, and then put together a bundle of services that addresses their needs. Sometimes we solve problems they're not even aware of. Given that, the chances of them changing carriers to save a penny a minute are pretty slim."

Among Value Call's success stories: putting together a phone package for a Tallahassee, Florida, radio station that needed to block

800-line calls from Tallahassee residents—while encouraging them from the rest of the state; and finding the exact service for a tele-marketing firm that wanted to make sure its employees were talking to customers, not their out-of-state relatives, without actually monitoring the calls.

CRAFT CUSTOM-MADE SOLUTIONS: THE SECOND MODEL OF TAILORING

In 1993, private-label jeans such as The Gap's own brand began to erode the denim-jeans market for the first time. The news was not lost on Levi Strauss & Co. For decades, the venerable San Francisco company had dominated the jeans market, selling through retailers whose loyalty it assumed. Now those retailers were giving aid and comfort to Levi Strauss & Co.'s competitors. That year, Levi Strauss & Co. initiated a costly, multiyear reorganization known as CSSC: Customer Service Supply Chain.

But how to get people out of The Gap and back into Levis?

Levi can offer customers something they can't get elsewhere. The company is tailoring its service, literally—Personal Pair Custom Fit Jeans for Women. The salesclerks take their customers' measurements and, in addition to those statistics, enter style numbers, color choices, and other specifications into a computer. When the salesclerk hits "Enter," she initiates production of a customized pair of jeans. Each pair costs $75, delivery guaranteed within three weeks. Do you think that the program will be a success? Just ask any woman how difficult it is to find a pair of jeans that really fits.

The Personal Pair Jeans for Women program is a classic example of the second model of tailoring, crafting custom-made solutions. It moves beyond AutoZone's product selection by offering products and services that are designed and built to meet the precise specifications of its customer, taking into account each and every curve of her body.

Sonoco Products Company's industrial-bulk-container division is another example. The entire outfit has won more than 70 awards for being a top-level supplier, and its growth rate is advancing 10 to 15 percent annually since its founding 96 years ago. Here again, success stems directly from the division's commitment to the personalized-customization tactic.

Suppose a plastics manufacturer needs a holding tank for its petroleum-based supplies. Sonoco investigates the company's specific situation. Its engineers check out the operation's location, the materials to be handled, and related environmental considerations. With that information, they work with the manufacturer's engineers to come up with the most cost-effective and operationally efficient container. If the plastics company has special materials requirements for a new shipping container, Sonoco designs, builds, and installs it.

Service companies are also finding ways to practice personalized customization, with impressive results for both customers and suppliers. CIGNA Retirement & Investment Services, for example, in its efforts to assure each corporation a carefully fitted solution, tailors its retirement benefit programs to each individual client. Jeananne Digan, manager of new business integration, states the case succinctly. "It's my job to know my clients. I have to be familiar with what they want, and I have to know them well enough to understand whether what they want is going to help them or not. If the very best retirement plan for a given company doesn't exist yet, it's my job to sit with the client and figure out how to design it. That's what I do: I sit with them until we've come up with a perfect plan that meets their needs."

Embellish the Core Product

Crafting custom-made solutions can open up a completely new way for a company to do business.

Since its founding in 1920, Pitney Bowes has dominated the postage-meter market. Only a handful of companies—Jell-O, Kleenex, and Coca-Cola, for instance—have seen their names enter the American lexicon. Pitney Bowes is a member of that select group. Over time, Pitney Bowes invested millions in research and development and expanded its product line by continuing to apply cutting-edge technology to increase the productivity and efficiency of other business processes as well. Take the highly competitive facsimile market, for instance.

Today a few dozen companies—including Sharp, Canon, Ricoh, Panasonic, and Xerox—fight for position in the low-end fax machine market. Pitney Bowes, which entered the facsimile business in 1982, has remained focused on high-end solutions designed to meet the unique needs of *Fortune* 1000 and midsized companies. This is reflected in their 47 percent share of the corporate fax market. Pitney Bowes has attained this lion's share by offering its customers the finest products and services tailored to corporate requirements. Recognizing that major companies need technology to respond to the individual needs of its users, Pitney Bowes looked for ways to enhance the effectiveness of its products. In addition to offering proprietary software that increases speeds and refines error correction capabilities (resulting in cost savings from reduced phone charges) and including labor-saving features such as delayed-send and broadcasting, Pitney Bowes is the only company that provides custom software solutions. These solutions address specific business challenges across a broad array of vertical markets and departments.

For example, customized software has been a tremendous value to the securities industry. An SEC mandate requires an archive copy of all customer transactions, many of which are conducted by fax. This could have meant a significant loss of time and money. Security firms needed an efficient way to secure transmitted information. In response to this challenge, Pitney Bowes engineers designed a system that sends messages to a protected archive system for storage. Only after the receipt of this archive copy is confirmed will the fax machine, the Pitney Bowes 9750, send the transaction to be processed. This solution has been installed at various securities companies, allowing them to adhere to SEC requirements while providing timely, accurate, and cost-effective customer response.

Another example, developed for a legal firm, can cross vertical markets to any company that receives a large volume of faxes. Originally, a person had to go through the pile of received faxes and sort them into individual transmissions. Aside from the time involved, human error sometimes caused confidential information to go to the wrong recipient. The solution was to have a tray loaded with colored paper feed the first page of a document. All subsequent pages would feed from another tray loaded with white paper. Now when a pile of faxes is received, the person sorting simply pulls the colored page and all following white pages. A new colored page indicates a new fax.

By partnering with its customers and learning how they work, Pitney Bowes is able to create networks that enhance business procedures while offering cost and labor savings as well. These networks, which can include custom software, are designed around the needs and requests of each individual customer. Corporations no longer feel that the integration of fax into their environments is limited by off-the-shelf technology. For Pitney Bowes, custom software has opened numerous avenues for new business.

Build Solutions from the Ground Up

A hardworking relative of mine, an upstanding woman now well into her 80s, responded to her children's every complaint—about everything from school to business to marriage—by declaring, "I never said it was going to be easy." The time has come for me to say the same— "I never said tailoring was going to be easy." It takes creative thinking; it might well include a lot of organizational restructuring; and it certainly will entail a heck of a lot of hard work. But as Degrémont, a division of the French company Lyonnaise des Eaux, illustrates, those rewards will more than compensate for the mighty efforts.

Degrémont is a French water-treatment company with purification plants in more than 40 countries. In many languages, Degrémont is the word that means water purification. In Egypt, for instance, one drinkable water drop out of two is purified with Degrémont systems. Overall growth of the Degrémont group in the past six years has exceeded 15 percent annually, to exceed $1 billion in 1995. Degrémont's far-reaching success is the direct result of its wise, long-term investments in difficult markets, understanding those markets as intimately as possible, and then following our second model, crafting tailor-made solutions—from top to bottom—to produce unrivaled results. Degrémont is a superb example of how far some companies are willing to go for their customers.

Each of the countries in which Degrémont operates has its distinctive culture, climate, language, standards for water purification, and regulatory environment. Within a country such as China— where Degrémont has built more than 30 plants—there are even regional differences. Some customers want clean drinking water, some want sewage treatment, some want industrial effluence cleanups. Virtually every aspect of every job is unique.

Degrémont copes with such challenges by learning about each country's needs long before it files its contract bids with them.

Degrémont stations people in prospective markets for years—sometimes as many as 10—to learn about conditions, culture, and potential problems, and to scout for possible partners as they did in Japan. By the time a local municipality or other organization sends out a request for proposal, Degrémont's advance team can facilitate swift delivery of a highly specific response. On more than one occasion, the company has a better understanding of the real geological, environmental, political, and financial issues than the customers themselves. This impressive feat accounts for Degrémont's penetration of notoriously difficult markets in Asia, the Middle East, and Latin America: China, Indonesia, Nigeria, and Argentina. Its intimate knowledge of a country or region allows Degrémont to deal responsibly with sensitive cultural and religious issues. Prospects and customers alike consider it a welcome guest, rather than a mistrusted outsider.

As decentralized as Degrémont's decision-making processes are, company communication is intensive, especially among engineers working on diverse projects around the world. The great body of their shared knowledge enables Degrémont to ground its tailoring in extremely broad experience. The lessons learned at a Norwegian sewage-treatment plant have come in handy as far away as Bali.

Customer-intimate companies don't aim to recoup all their costs and make a profit on every deal. Their perspective is the long haul, which, as Degrémont well knows, can be very long indeed. Finding the right solution for a customer in a particular region of a particular country requires considerable investment of time and money. They know that if they tap into the right markets, their investment will pay off handsomely.

Tailoring to a broad range of highly distinctive customers scattered in many countries often brings an unanticipated advantage: Diversification minimizes risk. Simultaneous operation in disparate environments—each with its own ups and downs—protects a company from vagaries of cyclical markets that boost results one year but drag them down the next. Such companies earn consistent raves from industry and investment analysts as well as from their customers. Their unwavering success traces its roots to tailoring total solutions: They anticipate customers' needs with years of observation and study in order to fit made-to-measure products and services, and broker resources to finance them as required.

TAKE THE CUSTOMER'S PROBLEM AWAY: THE THIRD MODEL OF TAILORING

When such companies as Degrémont and CIGNA tailor by designing solutions from the ground up, it appears that they've done as much as possible to custom-fit products and services. Degrémont not only custom builds water-purification plants around the world, it also negotiates contracts to manage the operation of those plants. It takes responsibility for keeping the systems up and running and overseeing suppliers and repair crews. Similarly, CIGNA administers all or some of the benefits packages it has designed for large customers, like United Technologies in Hartford, Connecticut. Such approaches bring us to the third and final model of tailoring.

The value proposition in the third tailoring model is "We'll do it all for you. We'll remove your problem by assuming the duties that trouble you." Such customer-intimate companies do for the customer what the customer can't or won't do itself. This final model of tailoring delivers big, broad solutions. Authentic customer intimacy—that in which a deep bond is created between supplier and customer—frequently leads to this kind of tailoring.

As we've already seen, Baxter International's tailoring for Massachusetts General Hospital brought that hospital's purchasing operations to a new level of efficiency. With its resources focused on caring for the sick—its real job—MGH no longer frets about the details of purchasing, delivery, and distribution.

Hospitals much smaller than MGH have reaped similar benefits from Baxter's programs. As mentioned earlier in this chapter, the Seton Medical Center in Daly City, California, saved almost $400,000 over two years by utilizing the PBDS program. PBDS is a service through which Baxter provides virtually all supplies needed for a surgical procedure in one customized package, eliminating the labor involved in ordering, receiving, and assembling numerous products individually. There is also no superfluous inventory in storage. North Broward Hospital in southern Florida forecasts savings of at least $5 million over the next five years. That figure, by the way, does not take into account a recent incident that highlighted an unforeseen benefit of Baxter's program. In 1995, when thieves broke into a hospital warehouse, they quickly fled, thwarted and confused. Ordinarily, the warehouse held more than $1 million of essential supplies. But, thanks to Baxter's takeover of supply and delivery functions, the thieves found nothing but bare shelves and empty containers.

Roadway Logistics Systems (ROLS), now known as Caliber Logistics, Inc., was founded in 1989 as a subsidiary of Roadway Services, Inc., now known as Caliber System, Inc. ROLS was in the "brains" business: to design and manage integrated distribution systems for its customers, who could then redirect their time, resources, and creative energy to their core activities.

At automotive plants where workers assemble a variety of models, Caliber Logistics' advanced computer system oversees and manages receipt of more than 1,400 parts from nearly 300 suppliers. Linking departments and tracking orders, Caliber Logistics assures that parts arrive exactly when needed: no shortages, overstocks, or oversights. The arrangement involves a tremendous amount of teamwork. Tom Escott, Caliber Logistics' vice president of sales and marketing, views the ideal relationship between supplier and customer as "a close, ongoing collaboration. There's got to be mutual respect and a sharing of responsibilities."

When cooperation along those lines pleases and impresses the customer, the two companies often find ways to expand and experiment with new forms of tailoring. Bill Jones, vice president of Caliber Logistics' transportation and business development, says that while managing the operation of one process for a company, Caliber Logistics naturally sees other areas where it could help. "In the beginning, companies—especially the ones that fear relying too heavily on a single supplier—tend to look at us as cross-eyed outsiders," Jones says. "But when we're successful, and the process is stabilized, companies are eager for us to look at other areas. After all, we can draw from eight years of experience spotting problems. Our customers realize it's natural for them to have one company assemble all the pieces to make the whole work."

Consider Outsourcing: The Tailored Approach

Companies have long been outsourcing accounting, advertising, public relations, and legal work. What is new and different in today's business world in the accomplishments just discussed is the degree of intimacy involved, the sharing of responsibilities, and—perhaps most significant—the mutual respect and trust.

The outsourcing model of tailoring is more relevant today than it was yesterday. And it's destined to stay relevant right into the next century. Businesses feel more pressure than ever before to streamline functions, compress operations, and cut fat wherever possible. In today's atmosphere of reduced staffs and higher expectations, outsourcing is essential to companies' staying focused on their critical processes and operating at maximum efficiency. Outsourcing makes companies less vulnerable to economic cycles and downturns. Until companies like Baxter International came to help them, few hospitals realized how much cash they had tied up in inventory management.

Outsourced processes that require sizable investments do generate major financial advantages. That's why there's a growing movement toward outsourcing information- and high-technology systems. Why buy and install your own elaborate computer system if another company can handle your problems with far greater operating efficiencies? Why spend the time trying to master new areas of functional expertise? Managing an outside supplier is often easier than managing staff—especially when inadequate experience hampers progress. The key, however, is intimacy. Everything depends on suppliers presenting their customers with the solutions that can come only from customer intimacy.

A CAVEAT OR TWO

In the midst of all this enthusiasm—and before we move on—it's only fair to point out that tailoring, like just about everything else in life, has some potential pitfalls. The best way to avoid the dangers is to know exactly what to look for.

In the introduction to this section of the book, I said that while it's essential for customer-intimate companies to focus on their customers, it's equally important for them to be self-aware. Part of knowing yourself is knowing both your strengths and your weaknesses, and knowing how to set limits. Large, powerful customers are likely to make large, powerful demands. All too often, a company finds itself pushed in a fruitless direction. Remember, no one model of tailoring has more intrinsic value than the others. Focus on what your company is able to deliver and on the model of tailoring that will create the most productive relationship with your customers. Learn to spot the difference between catering to a true customer need and accommodating unproductive idiosyncrasies.

A second, related danger is providing too much variety, which can send your costs skyrocketing and ultimately drive your customers to competitors. Sumitomo offers prospective house builders an impressive number of options, but not an unlimited number. Those limits help Sumitomo keep its prices so appealingly low. This is the rule: A multiplicity of models means complexity, and, ultimately, increased costs. Keep variety exciting, not excessive.

As for self-awareness, remember this rule: Tailor hard and innovatively, but don't be intimidated into taking on a job you can't perform well. Never forget your own identity and what you do best. Says John Foster, chairman and CEO of NovaCare, the rehabilitation services provider, "When you look at them closely, the organizations that survive all stand for something. And it's what they stand for that attracts members, customers, volunteers, contributors, whomever. If you look at your 10 favorite companies, I think you'll find that in addition to being leaders in their industries, they all have easily identifiable value sets. There's no question in my mind that those values come first, and the results follow in their path."

In more familiar words: Don't attempt to be all things to all people. Those who try to stand for everything end up standing for nothing. Use your self-knowledge as an essential tool in tailoring to your customer.

6 | THE COACHING ROUTE: GUIDE YOUR CUSTOMERS TOWARD BETTER RESULTS

As much as we love plants and flowers, the truth is, they can be a little intimidating. Their names are hard to pronounce and impossible to remember: cymbidium, longiflorum, cyclamen, bougainvillaea. Their variety is stupefying, their fragility daunting. On top of that, each seems to mean something special—but what? Quickly now, where do lilies "go"? The hospital or the funeral service? Are chrysanthemums festive enough for a 40th wedding anniversary, or are they too depressingly "autumnal"? As for roses, their colors seem to signify everything from grief to sexual ecstasy. You've got to be really careful with roses. Sometimes, it's easier just to buy chocolates.

Calyx & Corolla, the mail-order flower company, realized that it could do nothing to improve plants and flowers—nature has been fine-tuning that job for the past several million years. Its inspiration was to turn customers' embarrassment into opportunities.

C&C provides a number of services designed to make floral purchases simple, satisfying, and appealing. According to Ruth Owades, C&C founder, education is at the root of her business. "People hesitate to go into a store and confess that they don't know a lily from an orchid. It's a lot easier when you're on the phone and you have our illustrated catalog in front of you. Our staff is trained to ask tactful questions to help people get exactly what they want without feeling they're being judged. While we're at it, we encourage people to use flowers not only for special occasions, but as part of their everyday decor, the way many Europeans do."

Once customers receive C&C's product, they can call a toll-free number and talk to a "plant doctor" who might advise them to move ailing flowers or plants away from drafts or to a sunnier window.

Calyx & Corolla has adopted the second style of customer intimacy: coaching. The term captures the combination of encouragement and instruction that companies like C&C have found to be the surest route to customer closeness. Coaching companies change their customers' behaviors in order to get good results.

As in tailoring, I see three basic models of coaching. In the first, companies deal with problems of underutilized products or underexploited markets. The coaching company educates its customers to derive as much value from their purchases as possible. If you bought your VCR from a company that practices coaching, you not only know how to play movies, you can also record from your TV, program your recorder, and stop that annoying light that flashes 12:00.

In the second model, companies show their customers how to change the patterns or business processes in which they use goods and services. Witness Calyx & Corolla's attempt to direct customers to everyday, Euro-style use of plants and flowers. The coaching company is the engineer of change.

In the third model, companies go beyond showing their customers how to make better use of their products, beyond enhancing the processes in which they use the products. In this model, the customer-intimate company mentors its customer to build new business opportunities. In *The Discipline of Market Leaders,* we described how Cott Corporation, the Canadian soft-drink manufacturer, helped supermarkets such as Safeway establish their own private-label sodas. In one sense, Cott's product—the cola itself—was almost incidental to the total proposal: opening up new business ventures.

It's crucial to emphasize once again that, while these three models demand different levels of intimacy and involvement, no one model has more intrinsic value than the others. It's important to understand each before deciding which model or combination of models is most useful and appropriate for your business and your customers.

BRING OUT THE PRODUCT'S FULL BENEFITS: THE FIRST MODEL OF COACHING

For decades, when consumers bought baking soda they used it almost exclusively for leavening cakes, cookies, and breads, taking the occasional teaspoonful or two stirred into a glass of water to relieve indigestion. An inexpensive, effective, reliable product that few homes were without. Arm & Hammer had nothing to worry about, right? Wrong. With so few uses, a single box could easily last months, and as cake mixes gained popularity, it might last years.

Because Arm & Hammer couldn't improve the product itself, it decided to boost its value to customers by exploiting its versatility. It undertook an advertising campaign to educate consumers about all the myriad uses for that fine white powder sitting in their cabinet:

Add some to the bathwater on hot afternoons. Dump it down the drain to eliminate odors. Mix it with vinegar to clean the toilet bowl. Keep a box in the fridge to absorb sour smells. Toss some into the washing machine for brighter and fresher laundry. Arm & Hammer discovered and promoted even more possibilities, and sales jumped. Most American homes now stock several boxes: one with the flour and sugar, one in the bathroom, one in the back of the refrigerator, one near the cat's litter box. Today, consumers consider baking soda an essential ingredient of daily household maintenance.

This fairly straightforward illustration demonstrates the first model of coaching. In educating customers about all the potential—and previously unexploited—uses of its product, a company increases the product's value to consumers and propels sales. In all three models, coaches act as educators and trainers, but here, education and training are their primary functions.

Another expression of this variety of coaching is providing manuals and instructional materials that are concise, readable, and easy to follow. This should be a standard procedure for every manufacturer, but an astonishing number of products are underutilized because the instruction manuals are indecipherable to anyone but cunning children and other experts. If you own a VCR, a computer, or a host of gadgets, gizmos, and technologically advanced appliances, you know exactly what I mean. Most of us have neither the energy nor the inclination to read the manuals five or six times, so we learn to use only a fraction of a product's potential.

Once they take care of such basics, companies can go farther—much farther—to educate and inform their customers. Look at Home Depot: Professionally trained, highly experienced salespeople in every department—plumbing, carpentry, gardening, and so on—offer patient, comprehensive counsel to do-it-yourselfers eager to get the most out of their purchases.

Or look at SKF: When that Swedish manufacturer realized how

few of its worldwide customers knew how to install and maintain its ball bearings, it started to offer three-day seminars that included on-the-job training to help customers optimize performance of SKF's products. A traveling team of SKF educators and trainers spends the year on the road, visiting work sites and factories to make sure customers are up-to-the-minute on every new feature and function.

Or look at Quad/Graphics: The respected printer invites its customers—publishers of popular magazines and retail catalogs—to spend time at its CAMP/Quad. For two to three days—between recreational activities and fine dining—customers immerse themselves in the company's technology, learning about the latest advances in imaging, printing, and finishing. "The more they learn about us," customer service manager Pamela Rostagno says, "the better for both of us. A lot of art directors and circulation managers have no idea how we even get ink onto paper. Once we introduce them to our technology, they can figure out how to make it work best for them."

Optimizing your products' benefits is the goal of all coaching. Devotees of the first coaching model do this by instructing customers in the product's every use and application.

The Product Isn't the Problem

A brochure for Ceridian Corporation's Employer Services division features enthusiastic quotes from satisfied customers. Check out this blurb from the operations accounting manager at Lamonts, a popular clothing retailer: "Our sincere thanks for your visit to conduct our annual payroll system review and update. It gave us the perfect opportunity to learn more about new features so that we can utilize them more effectively. It was a very productive meeting and we thank you for your continued support and assistance."

Not exactly poetry, but music to the ears of Ceridian managers.

It affirms what Ceridian does superbly and what many others in the same and related industries have yet to match: comprehensive coaching of customers in the use and integration of its products. Ceridian makes sophisticated software for human resources information management and also provides integrated payroll and tax filing services and more; but what it sells—to quote once again from its brochure—is a formidable combination of "start-up services and ongoing support." Ceridian customers buy both the product and the assurance that they'll know how to use every facet of it.

Ceridian is coaching so successfully, you'd think every company would take the same path. Some have tried and failed, and it's worth considering the reasons for their difficulties. What may be holding them back, ironically, is their intense concentration on building superior products. In *The Discipline of Market Leaders* we call this "focus on product leadership." Companies that adore technology and the minutiae of design have a tendency to overlook the possibility that their customers may not understand what their products actually do (or don't do). They compound that problem when they decide that their customer is insufficiently appreciative of their wonderful product, or that perhaps the customer is just downright dumb. Dealing with design and technical-performance issues looks easy compared with trying to psych out and power up a confused, glum customer.

Managers and designers with a product-leadership mind-set no doubt shrink from what Ceridian's position in the marketplace seems to suggest: The development of technology takes a backseat to coaching customers in its use. From the customer's perspective, it's irrelevant who actually designs, manufactures, and markets the stuff. All a customer cares about is whether the technology works properly and delivers the promised results.

Between those two perspectives, an opportunity gapes wide open, an opportunity for customer intimacy: The opportunity, I maintain, for the rest of this century and beyond. As Michael Borman, a

Ceridian product manager, points out, even when a company meets the technological criteria to be a player, the biggest concern of both current and potential customers will be "the service-related issues: implementing, training, and ongoing support of their systems."

It makes sense, doesn't it? If you can't understand how to unlock the features of your new software, it's useless. You wouldn't invest in that inaccessible potential any more than you'd pay the rent on a 2,000-square-foot apartment if half of it was closed off. Think of coaching as a way to open up doors—not only for your customer, but for yourself as well.

Coach with Outsiders' Assistance

Ceridian's success, and the lessons we can glean from it, clearly point out the opportunity—even the necessity—of coaching. But suppliers might logically ask whether they want to develop coaching as part of their main business or enlist the assistance of an external consultant, middleman, or intermediary to take on the role.

Certainly there's no shortage of available resources. As customers face more complex products, systems for integrating the products into their own processes grow increasingly complicated. Myriad businesses have sprung up to fill the instructional gaps left by product-focused suppliers. The new services are directed toward training, education, and knowledge transfer. In any computer store, Wal-Mart, or Barnes & Noble you'll find a large and rapidly expanding collection of books, audiotapes, videos, and CD-ROMs that instruct consumers in the uses and applications of software, information systems, and other technologically advanced products. More than 17 million copies from the ... *For Dummies* series of computer-related instructional books have been sold worldwide. This suggests that even prominent and famously user-friendly software companies don't speak plainly enough for some buyers. SAP AG, a German company that's taken the software market by storm, offers customers the same level of support service as Ceridian, but relies almost exclusively on outsiders to do their coaching.

In 1972, several ex-IBMers founded SAP to pursue their vision for computer systems that would integrate management of manufacturing, sales, finances, and human resources. Their ideas evolved into SAP's R/3 client/server software, a product that promotes a cooperative work environment by enabling information sharing among departments and speeding up business processes. SAP's share of the worldwide market for such software climbed to 31 percent by 1994, bringing in roughly $1 billion in revenues.

To its dismay, soon after its product's introduction in 1992, SAP discovered that customers were running into problems. The payoff for embracing SAP's R/3 technology was limited to corporations that could streamline or reengineer their work processes. SAP quickly recognized the urgency of the problem when its top customers expressed their disappointment and pressed for better training and education. SAP's strengths were its engineering, R&D, and product development. SAP knew it wasn't sufficiently rich in the resources and skills it would need to train its customers and potential customers.

Instead of taking the time to develop training resources internally, SAP's managers decided to forge intimate working relationships with information and integration systems consultants. It set up a program, Logo Partners, to provide SAP customers with strategic services. The 14 Logo Partners include Arthur Andersen, Deloitte & Touche, Price Waterhouse, and other Big Six accounting firms; a variety of prominent consulting and systems-oriented service firms including CSC Consulting, EDS, and CAP Gemini; and such technology vendors as Hewlett-Packard, IBM's consulting group, and Siemens Nixdorf. The Logo Partners coach SAP's customers in the design and implementation of reengineering efforts. When difficulties arise, as they inevitably do, the customers call Logo Partners for help. The result is that customers are able to reap the full benefits of the technology and realize all the gains the designers imagined.

The number of SAP customers that Arthur Andersen and Price Waterhouse alone have trained suggests the scale of the coaching effort and confirms the software's popularity. *Fortune* magazine reports that those two firms added a thousand new consultants in 1995 simply to accommodate the exploding demand for SAP software coaches.

By forming alliances with Logo Partners instead of undertaking that effort on its own, SAP not only relieved itself of an enormously expensive and painful expansion, it also ensured that its customers are getting some of the best-trained, most qualified, and experienced consultants and teachers in the world. Working in close cooperation, SAP and its allies deliver the best total solution. Without that customer-intimate approach, SAP's core product would have been immeasurably less valuable and, undoubtedly, less successful.

SHAPE UP THE CUSTOMER'S USAGE PROCESS: THE SECOND MODEL OF COACHING

We've already seen how Levi Strauss & Co. grabbed a distinct market advantage by making new use of High Point Chemical's tailoring efforts to create a variation on the stonewashed look. Then it was up to retailers to promote and sell the new products. No matter how appealing the apparel is, it's not likely to sell if an inexperienced or disorganized retailer sticks it in a back corner of his store or if he incompetently orders the wrong quantities of the most sought-after styles and sizes. If retailers aren't reaching the end customers, they're obviously going to suffer, and so, ultimately, will the manufacturer.

To address this issue, Levi Strauss & Co. installed an electronic data interchange network, LeviLink. LeviLink connects the manufacturing division of the company with its point-of-sale merchants. The information system helps the manufacturing end coordinate retailers' stock management and reordering. Merchandise is on the shelves when customers want it. LeviLink helps merchandisers display goods to their best advantage, tells them when to rotate seasonal merchandise, and suggests the right times for markdowns and clearance sales.

By helping its retailers change their business processes, Levi Strauss & Co. is pursuing the second model of coaching. Levi Strauss & Co. is the engineer of change for retailers: the very definition of this model. But wait a minute: Does that approach violate the old adage that the customer is always right? You bet. The customer isn't always right. Sometimes the customer's processes are unresponsive, outdated, and counterproductive. And, remember, when the end customer's needs aren't being met, suppliers and manufacturers all down the line—from production to distribution—suffer.

To some degree, product use is always a function of people's behavior within a larger context. Therefore, to meet coaching's goal—getting the best results from products or services—your guidance must often extend well beyond the product's narrow use into new ways of thinking, planning, and organizing. Backed by the wealth of information and advanced analyses of the LeviLink database, Levi Strauss & Co. provides retailers of all sizes new opportunities for improvement.

Become the Customer's Trusted Advisor

Staples National Advantage (SNA), a division of Staples, the chain of discount office-supply superstores based in Massachusetts, has built a tremendously successful business reshaping its customers' procurement processes. In 1995, SNA had 125 customers, some 90 percent of whom were committed to purchasing more than $1 million in office products annually. All 125 of them have, in the words of Tara Santry, vice president of sales, "forged a strategic relationship with us in which we do more than merely supply goods." Although Staples believes its prices are highly competitive, the SNA division isn't interested in customers whose only concern is price. "We want people who have a perspective that makes them open to change," Santry elaborates. "Those are the customers we seek out because we know those are the ones we'll be able to work with most effectively."

SNA changes the customers' processes in three areas. One: SNA trains customers accustomed to local, scattershot buying to adopt a national approach, using hard figures to prove that the catch-as-catch-can method is wasteful and costly. Two: SNA encourages customers to switch from paper-based to electronic ordering processes. Three: SNA trains its customers to stop purchasing for inventory—a system that calls for stockpiling and reordering supplies as they dwindle. The just-in-time (JIT) delivery SNA endorses reduces the expense of maintaining storerooms, monitoring inventories, and risking theft. Companies that use JIT are certain to have the right products available at exactly the right moment.

Coaching customers through such changes requires an individualized approach. And an individualized approach begins with comprehensive understanding of the mechanics and economics of a customer's day-to-day operations. Staples recognized that it would never be given the latitude to study its customers' premises unless customers believed that SNA's goal was to help them. "If you're viewed as a sales rep, just selling price, you keep butting your head against the door without ever getting inside," reports Shira Goodman, marketing vice president. "The only time our customers invite us to sit at the table with them is when they view us as a consultant or a trusted adviser. When we do sit down with them, we're not talking about office products. We're talking about the entire cycle of commitment, acquisition, and how they pay for goods."

Just as Ceridian Employer Services' success is linked more closely to its service than to its software, Staples National Advantage has established itself as a trusted business adviser. Its operational excellence, grounded in Staples' highly streamlined and cost-efficient retail chain, is surely a great advantage. But office supplies sometimes seem almost incidental to the value Staples National Advantage creates by coaching its selected group of customers. Customers recognize the beneficial results across the board.

Explore New Ways of Operating

In 1990, Xerox introduced the DocuTech Production Publisher, an extraordinary tool that drastically changed the nature and capabilities of copy machines. Instead of making an electrostatic image of a printed page and making duplicates of it, the DocuTech scans each document to create a digital image. This image is immediately reproducible or can be stored in memory for later copying or printing. Stored images, unlike photographic pictures, can be wired to locations around the globe and the recipients can reproduce them at their leisure. Furthermore, people can easily enhance, edit, and modify such digital images infinitely with no loss of quality or clarity.

Xerox had absolute confidence that its machine would ultimately prove invaluable to a large number of its customers. But they also recognized that before they introduced the product to the market, users would need help to learn how to make the most of its capabilities. Xerox assembled a consulting team to work directly with those customers that are heavy users of complex documents. The team introduced the customers to the expeditious DocuTech process of creating and disseminating text. The effort paid off. Since 1990, DocuTech has seen annual sales of about $1 billion.

Boeing, the aircraft manufacturer, writes customized maintenance manuals for each plane. This painfully laborious process requires constant alteration and updating, and—fortunately for all of us—incredibly stringent accuracy. Xerox recognized that Boeing's manual writers could really take advantage of DocuTech. Xerox studied Boeing's process of producing manuals. Working side by side with Boeing's engineers and information specialists, Xerox learned all the specific requirements and restrictions and designed a new methodology that incorporated DocuTech systems. Like Staples National Advantage, Xerox first earned the respect and trust of its customer and then guided it through the intricate changeover from old to new approaches.

Sell Productivity, Not Products

In the words of Vice President and General Manager Jeff Immelt, GE Plastics' most important product is "customer productivity." The GE subsidiary uses a three-pronged approach to deliver this product. First, it organizes industry-specific teams that focus on such specific product lines as connectors, printers, and automotive instrument panels. Those teams work closely with customers to develop innovative products and technologies. Once they perfect product prototypes, they help customers design manufacturing and delivery processes that keep costs low and productivity high. But the final step is most relevant to the issue of coaching: They organize follow-up teams that go into customers' plants and help straighten out any problems that may arise.

In 1995, GE Plastics had more than 100 of those productivity teams in the field. For customers committed to cost down, GE Plastics can provide a joint team approach. All team members are trained to troubleshoot, not only in the use of GE Plastics products, but in a wide range of related business and technology processes as well. Rather than imposing ready-made solutions, they work with their customers. They aim to create mutual trust and to understand the exact nature of each customer's problem in the context of its specific systems and culture. "We start out by questioning them," explains Immelt. "Are they having scrap problems? Trouble with yield? Is there some glitch with their inventory turns? But we use a lot of our own observations, too, and when we start the process of designing a solution, we have hundreds of experiences from which to draw."

This system generates savings and benefits for both GE Plastics and its customers. For the customer, the rewards can be rich indeed. According to Immelt, the coaching program produced customer savings of $68 million in 1995. Under its productivity teams' contracts, GE usually gets value for these savings through share or price.

"My notion," says Immelt, "is that selling is dead. These days, account managers have to be customer-productivity experts. That's what we're really selling. All of our managers know process skills. Our payoff is that the customer gets better value for what we do. We get value, but more important, we get more business in the end. Everyone wins with this approach."

BREAK NEW GROUND WITH THE CUSTOMER: THE THIRD MODEL OF COACHING

In an atmosphere of heavy competition, no soft drinks are more threatening to big-name contenders than the once-inconsequential private-label sodas and the recently introduced Virgin Cola. Cott Corporation of Canada is definitely celebrating: In the three years ending January 1995, the company achieved a compound annual growth rate in sales of approximately 100 percent. Cott is under contract to manufacture both Virgin Cola—the latest enterprise of Richard Branson, owner of Virgin Atlantic Airways—and J. Sainsbury's Classic Cola, the largest private-label brand in Great Britain. What's more, Cott can proudly lay claim to having assisted both successful brands into existence.

Cott exemplifies the third model of coaching: a supplier assisting its customers into new business ventures, thereby enlarging its own market. By working with Richard Branson and the brand-name magic of Virgin Atlantic, Cott is able to increase demand for its product without draining profits and creative energy in an all-out marketing effort. Initially, Cott supplied Virgin Atlantic with syrups and carbonated water. With Cott's assistance, Virgin has moved into a new product line that has proven hugely successful for both. This is the third model of coaching in action: The supplier as venture mentor.

MBNA Corp. is one of the fastest-growing issuers of credit cards in the United States; only the Goliath Citibank ranks above it in bank-card outstandings. Founded in 1982, MBNA had more than 18 million VISA and MasterCard customers by 1995. And those are not just any customers: MBNA can justifiably crow about the affluence of its customer base and its favorable rate of uncollectable loans. During the third quarter of 1995, the company had the sixth-lowest write-off rate among the 21 largest credit-card issuers. What is the secret to the success of this firm?

It isn't rock-bottom pricing. At about 16 percent, MBNA's interest rates are higher than some of the single-digit rates offered by some of its competitors. MBNA's rise to industry prominence is a result of its purveyance of affinity-program credit cards. Here's how it works: MBNA approaches an organization—the Sierra Club, for example—and coaches it into entering the credit-card business. The Sierra Club offers its members a Sierra Club VISA or MasterCard and earns .5 percent of all its members' credit-card purchases. The end-customers' credit cards display their affinity with the environmental group and make an automatic and cost-free contribution to its coffers. In 1994, the Sierra Club earned approximately $400,000 from its affinity card. MBNA works hard to find the customers it wants and focuses on keeping them.

The company has successfully created affinity cards for over 41,000 organizations including college alumni associations nationwide, fans of the Baltimore Orioles, the National District Attorney's Association, and even members of Britain's Rolls-Royce Enthusiasts Club.

REALITY CHECKS

Throughout this chapter, we've looked at companies that use coaching to create enormous benefits for themselves and their customers. Some companies believe that while they manufacture superior products, their most vital asset is their ability to educate, inform, and inspire their customers. I would be remiss if I didn't spend at least a few paragraphs discussing some of the potholes and pitfalls to look out for.

➤ Customer-intimate companies have to stay ahead of the customers they coach. Nothing's more embarrassing for a teacher than being unable to answer a student's question. Customer-intimate companies must continuously educate themselves about all aspects of their customers' businesses: expansion plans, setbacks, executives, personnel, the industry as a whole, the regulatory climate, even events half a world away that may have an impact. Customer loyalty has to be earned and re-earned. That's a difficult challenge: Repeating big wins, say, a spectacular money-saving process overhaul, is rare. It's equally important—and not necessarily easier—to deliver a growing mountain of small, day-to-day suggestions.

Fortunately, customer-intimate companies have a powerful weapon in their battle to stay ahead of their customers: collective wisdom. Through their dealings with customers in a variety of fields, they build a body of knowledge from which they can always draw sustenance. The suppliers always end up with wider experience, deeper understanding, and greater potential to lead.

➤ A company must never want for well-trained coaches, especially when it is introducing highly promising, potentially profitable products. SAP's triumphs caused bottlenecks in its coaching abilities, making the company's further growth rocky at times. Its solution—forging alliances—was bold and innovative, and delivered results when necessary: immediately.

➤ Choose customers wisely. The idea of turning away customers can be especially unattractive to start-ups and struggling companies, but in some respects, it's more important to fledgling companies than it is to better-established enterprises. Start-ups have to build credibility from scratch, and customers approach them more warily. A struggling company risks being written off by customers. They're not likely to earn a second chance.

In coaching, where shared goals and personal relationships based on mutual respect are essential to progress, choosing the right customer is particularly important. Few sports fans need to be told how incompatibility between coaches and players reduces chances for a winning season. Coaches must seize responsibility for pointing out any incompatibilities before they lead to disaster.

"In our business," says NovaCare chairman John Foster, "there are more customers than we have staff and management to serve. Therefore, we must always be confident that the relationships we develop can flourish and be highly productive.... If a prospective customer doesn't subscribe to a value set identical or similar to ours, it's unlikely that we'll have a successful customer relationship. It's best for us to point that out, rather than wait to have it pointed out to us."

➤ The basic equipment for successful business coaching is always complete knowledge of the customer and a deep understanding of the customers' problems. Good business coaches need not be able to perform all the tasks they recommend to a customer, but they must use intuition, imagination, and intellect to enter their customer's worlds. They must be able to see problems and possible solutions from their customers' point of view. Without that fundamental customer-intimate perspective, coaches are destined to find themselves stumbling, rather than leading the way, through the dark.

7 | THE PARTNERING ROUTE: INNOVATE—AND INTEGRATE— WITH YOUR CUSTOMER

Johnson Controls is the world's largest just-in-time provider of automotive seating "systems"—not only the seats but all the straps, bolts, and contouring devices that go with seats these days. Their client list is impressive, to say the least: Ford, General Motors, Chrysler, Toyota, Honda, Nissan, Mercedes, Volkswagen, Rover, and Renault. More to the point, the company is also a leading practitioner of our third way to customer intimacy—partnering.

Let's flesh out that abstraction with an example. Chrysler's close brush with death in the 1980s made it recognize, on penalty of ruin, that as a massive, vertically integrated organization it could not retain its position in today's automobile market. Today's customer demands ever more value from a new vehicle: More innovations, higher quality, faster delivery—all for a better price. Chrysler couldn't meet such demands alone. The company had to share the creativity and risk across its entire supply chain.

Johnson Controls was equal to the challenge—and more. It didn't deliver just seats—or even seating "systems." For instance, with Chrysler's compact Neon of 1994, Johnson took responsibility for everything: product planning and styling, design engineering, source control, and assembly. Day after day, Johnson's engineers worked with Chrysler's engineering teams to assure the new processes would deliver the form, fit, and functions that the two teams deemed appropriate.

Moreover, as the supplier of some 80 percent of the Neon's seating components, it was Johnson Controls, not Chrysler, that integrated the system development with Chrysler's other outside suppliers, orchestrating each contribution to guarantee a no-surprises product rollout. Johnson employees and suppliers alike prepared for the challenge by taking a "Quest" training program. Everyone focused on quality, cost containment, and deliverability to exceed Chrysler's expectations at each step. Johnson integrated the just-in-time sequence at its new manufacturing plant with next-door-neighbor Chrysler's own manufacturing process: It delivered its seating systems ready for installation, within two hours of Chrysler's order.

The relationship between Johnson Controls and Chrysler exemplifies our third, most challenging style of customer intimacy. I call this model partnering. In partnering, supplier and customer agree, "We will create results together." Partnering is more intricate than tailoring, which has the supplier finding the best solution and does not require the customer to change its usual business practices. And partnering is also more intricate than coaching, in which the supplier is the knowledgeable mentor who leads its customer to better performance through new business practices. In partnering, supplier and customer together take responsibility for finding the most productive solutions, changing their processes, their practices, and their behavior in coordinated pursuit of mutual benefit. It requires unusual levels of trust, a virtual integration of supplier and customer who, together, focus on the common good.

Chrysler's rigorous collaboration with Johnson Controls Automotive led to a better result than anything they could have devised on their own. And, as we saw in Chapter 3, Johnson Controls has benefited as well.

Full collaboration with its customers has been Johnson Controls' secret of success over the last decade. And as CEO James Keyes insists, full collaboration will, in the decades to come, continue to be the secret of its success. In the past, the company had concentrated on simple assembly, but as its customers began to subcontract certain processes, Keyes pushed to take on more responsibility. He aimed to win more business by adding more services. In Keyes' words, the company worked to become "a system supplier rather than a component supplier." That's when it began to site new plants adjacent to its customers' manufacturing facilities—both domestic and international—to smooth the integration of their jointly developed systems.

The capital expense of such a commitment is huge. In 1995 Johnson Controls put 10 new plants in Europe alone. Automakers know they can rely on Johnson to deliver results, and they are willing to pay for it. "Over the four-year period 1996-1999," Keyes points out, "we will be adding $1.6 billion in annual sales volume to our $2.9 billion base—business that has been awarded for the model years beginning in 1995, 1996, 1997, 1998."

And what of the decades to come?

"During the 1980s," Randi Somma, vice president of sales and marketing, says, "we couldn't have predicted what Johnson Controls would look like today; we knew only that we'd be structured around our clients needs. The same is true about the next decade. We cannot say where we will head; we can say only that as the global market continues to demand increased value, Johnson Controls will continue to be the kind of partner every automaker will find trustworthy."

Whose Job Is This Anyway?

Lots of people talk about "partnering." Like "family," it's a term people love to use in every sort of context. Even the Merrill Lynch salesperson who interrupts your Saturday morning to sell you some stocks may call his invasion of privacy an offer of partnership.

But, to Johnson Controls, true partnering means something far more exact—and exacting. It calls for full and open collaboration: both parties working together to find the best solutions to commonly defined problems. It means integration: no fail-safe process redundancies on either side. Most fearsome, it means interdependence, a mutual commitment to "hang together, or be hanged separately," as Benjamin Franklin said before signing the Declaration of Independence. The parties face the challenges and share the rewards, together.

Together, the partners decide who does what best. In some cases, the supplier is more capable and better prepared. In others, the customer is in the better position to add value. In still other cases, the optimal arrangement is to handle the task together. A true partnership performs like a great basketball team. All the team members know what each one does best, and everyone knows when to pass the ball to a teammate.

That clear understanding of one another's strengths, weaknesses, and rhythms—and the subsequently appropriate assignment of responsibilities—radically reduces the friction in traditional arm's-length relationships. It eliminates the talking, checking, and worrying. Partners are positioned to streamline communications and avoid second guessing. Like every winning team, customers and suppliers who collaborate effectively come to see themselves as nearly a single entity. They will create better designs, processes, and products than either could create alone.

As with coaching and tailoring, there are three ways to pursue partnering. In the first model, suppliers and customers work jointly to design new products or services, drawing from their respective areas of expertise. In the second, they synchronize aspects of their operations, usually to assure prompt and efficient delivery of the jointly designed product or service. In the third, supplier and customer integrate their business processes: The two jointly redesign their operating models to create entirely new ways of working together.

Again, as with coaching and tailoring, no one model is by definition "better" than the others. The model of partnering that works best depends on each individual customer. What differentiates the three models of partnering, however, is how many suppliers successfully move from the first to the second to the third, from joint design to synchronization to integration—as a partnership ripens over time. Collaboration enhances trust, and that allows for still more collaboration and continually improving results. We have seen that work for Johnson Controls, and we shall see Nypro, the innovative plastics-injection molding company we first met in Chapter 1, enjoying similar success.

COLLABORATE ON DESIGN: THE FIRST MODEL OF PARTNERING

The plastics-injection molding business was "cheap and dirty" in the mid-80s, according to Nypro CEO Gordon Lankton. With entry costs low, tens of thousands of small suppliers battled one another for small pieces of business. They competed on cost, so Lankton decided to take a different tack—and along the way he discovered customer intimacy. Determined to move away from run-of-the-mill injection molding, Lankton and his team started looking for the handful of more sophisticated customers that would benefit from state-of-the-art molding processes. Lankton would make partners of those customers—and together, they would develop products and processes for a collaborative future.

It paid off for both Nypro and such customers as Vistakon, a division of Johnson & Johnson. The specialty producer of optical lenses that correct astigmatism had sales that had plateaued at $20 million. But when Vistakon's president got a tip about a new and much less expensive lens manufacturing technique that had been developed in Copenhagen, he recognized the commercial opportunity, bought the patent rights, and set out to create what would become Acuvue, the world's first, and most successful, disposable contact lens.

When they first started to work with Vistakon the people at Nypro had some doubts about the new project, Lankton admits. On the plus side, they knew Johnson & Johnson's reputation for fostering new ideas and developing them quickly. But Vistakon had set the standards very high. To make Acuvue safe, precision was paramount. The specifications were extraordinary—far beyond the capability of any existing plastic injection system. Both high-volume and low-cost manufacturing were unequivocally required goals to make Acuvue affordable. Neither company had the knowledge nor capabilities to meet those challenges: They had to find their way together.

It was also difficult for the two to establish mutual trust. Vistakon, after all, was betting its future on a new vendor. And Nypro hesitated to share details of its process innovation for fear those details would find their way to its competitors. Once the engineers and designers from the two companies began to plan the project, the two groups realized there would be no innovation without uncensored complete sharing of knowledge, insight, and inspiration. Thanks to their collaboration, they jointly created a process breakthrough—injection molding machines that met higher specifications at a lower cost than had ever been possible before.

But Nypro's partnering with Vistakon extended beyond the development of the molding system. Together the two companies refined the process: Customer-improvement teams from both companies met formally every six weeks or so. Today, the two companies have far wider, informal connections. Collaboration stretches from the engineering department to the loading dock to senior management.

Results? Since 1989, Nypro's automated system has manufactured more than two billion defect-free plastic molds for Vistakon. Consequently Vistakon has eliminated its own incoming inspections entirely, and has reduced its customer service costs as well. Vistakon is now a giant in its industry, with more than 40 percent of the U.S. market. Nypro, for its part, has created a new industry standard, as well as partnering skills it continues to use with other customers, as we shall see later in this chapter.

Joint process design partnering is not always so intricate or demanding, however, nor does it always require constant, day-to-day intimacy. Sometimes, as I have explained, it can be as simple as partners asking, "Who should do this job?"

Focus on the Customer's Customer

As supplier and customer collaborate on a joint design—be it product, service, or process—both parties to the partnership experience an interesting metamorphosis. As they learn to work together, focused on the common search for results, the lines and distinctions between them start to blur. The customer becomes a full-fledged member of the supplier's design team, perhaps, or the supplier moves its product development efforts from its own lab into the lab of its customer. As GE Plastics worked in partnership with Delphi Interior & Lighting Systems (Delphi-I), a GM component supply division, to develop the revolutionary Super Plug—an automotive door module that combines the 60 parts of a conventional car door in a single module—engineers said the partnership was so close they often didn't know who worked for which company. "We could have swapped paychecks," one engineer marveled.

Delphi-I had needed a breakthrough. As the former Inland Fisher guide division, it had been part of what used to be GM's Automotive Components Group. In February 1994, with its new name, it took on a new challenge. As Delphi-I, it had to compete for GM's business like any other supplier for GM, but it had to diversify, too: Fifty percent of its sales had to come from other automakers. Delphi-I handled its new challenge well thanks to the technologies, materials, and processes the company had designed during its five-year collaboration with GE Plastics.

The Super Plug is an elegant solution to a complex problem. To include all the door components—wiring harnesses, door handles, window guidance channels, stereo speaker, electric motor, and so forth—in a single plastic piece, its designers created a new gas-assisted injection-molding process as well as a new resin designed for the new application.

"The development of the Super Plug was a critical step in providing next-generation part technology for our customers," Barbara Sanders, director of Delphi-I's engineering/advanced-development group, points out.

"We did it all in partnership all the way," Jeff Immelt, vice president and general manager of GE Plastics, adds. "Partnering allows us to leverage the expertise we have in materials with the expertise the customer has in design to get the maximum impact.

"We started together," Immelt says, "by working through the mechanical design for a manufacturing assembly. We asked, How many parts can we reduce? How many assembly steps can we reduce? What's the optional material?" The two groups looked at material specifications, manufacturing techniques, design assistance, and assembly ergonomics. Each brought considerable expertise to the project. Delphi-I brought unique skills in design and manufacturing-process creation, while GE Plastics was expert at materials development and molding systems. Immelt was impressed at just how much Delphi-I knew about leading edge plastics technology. "Those people actually know something about how to use our plastics to make their car better. And to do it speedier. And at lower cost."

What united the two companies was their journey toward a common goal. Delphi-I, in effect, was no longer GE Plastics' customer. They both were aiming for the same customers—automakers who would buy their jointly designed and manufactured product.

The result was impressive—the Super Plug offered reduction in the number of required parts, lower weight, lower cost per part, and shorter development and assembly time. Conventionally made doors have dozens of pieces that have to be bolted, riveted, or welded into place. The Super Plug is a single piece, snapped into place with just six fasteners. Tested prior to delivery, Super Plug delivers reliably high quality and drastically reduces risk of product rejection. It cuts warranty costs, eliminates squeaks and rattles, and even helps absorb motor noise.

Introduced in March of 1995, the Super Plug took the market by storm. "A revolution in the way automotive components are designed and assembled," *Ward's Auto World* called it. Barbara Sanders reports hearing from interested potential OEM customers from "all over the world."

The Super Plug is just the first jointly designed product of the carefully nourished partnership. Having figured out how to make simple component modules for automotive doors, GE Plastics and Delphi-I now are looking to leverage their new gas-assisted injection molding expertise to create other interior component systems, starting with instrument panels.

Which company will reap the benefits of their ongoing innovation? As in every true partnership, they both will. And so will the auto industry customers and the consumers who drive their cars.

SYNCHRONIZE YOUR OPERATIONS: THE SECOND MODEL OF PARTNERING

Partnering, as we have seen, is not a transaction or one-shot exchange between supplier and customer. It is a relationship that ripens over time. Facing a design challenge and finding the answer together usually produces more than an innovative solution to a specific problem. The process also creates the best possible launching pad for expanded and evermore productive collaboration.

The logical step for companies that are successful at partnering in design is to proceed to operational partnering. The goal of this next model is to streamline and refine the partners' jointly designed solution. Their relationship will evolve as they continually share their experiences and knowledge about what does and doesn't work.

Once again, Nypro is in the forefront.

We saw how Nypro used joint design partnering to develop defect-free plastic molds with contact lens maker Vistakon, and how Nypro developed partnering skills it could offer to other, potential customers. Among those customers is Abbott Laboratories, a diversified health-care company based in Illinois.

The two companies initiated that partnership, too, around a joint design challenge: to create a new plastic blood-test pack and the manufacturing process to produce it. The results were impressive: They were able to produce a new product of lower cost and higher quality, at a product-defect rate that, for the last 45 million of the total 100 million produced, held at zero. Nypro and Abbott attained their notable results by moving their collaboration beyond joint design of the manufacturing process to shared supervision of its ongoing operation.

Information was the key. They synchronized technology and integrated systems to give each company electronic access to one another's computer data. Nypro tied the control processes of its manufacturing systems into Abbott's, giving Abbott direct real-time access to information on the blood pack production process, which allowed Abbott's engineers to monitor output and statistical process control performance. Abbott, in turn, tied Nypro directly to its customer order information. Besides enhancing their mutual comfort and the value of their relationship, that open exchange of vital information gave both customer and supplier a platform for their continuing joint search for product, process, and cost improvements.

Make Teamwork Work

There are two crucial aspects of successful joint operational partnering. Supplier and customer must synchronize their information and technology, and each needs to designate certain of its employees to work on cooperating teams. Still, even with those efforts, this second model of partnering, like all customer intimacy, depends on making teamwork work, day after day and year after year.

John Foster, the CEO of NovaCare, keeps a simple sign in his office. "Relationships determine results," it reads. But Foster has learned during his 10-year partnership with National Health Care Affiliates, Inc. (NHCA) that it's far easier to hang a sign than to forge and maintain connections.

NHCA, a 45-unit home-nursing chain, became a NovaCare

customer through Foster's acquisition of InSpeech, NHCA's decade-long supplier of contract therapists. But the relationship nearly ended before it began. "NHCA represented about 20 percent of our total business," Foster remembers. "It was in the process of canceling our contracts. Service was poor, and with the change of ownership, promises weren't being kept. We realized that the key people throughout our organization had to develop relationships with their counterparts at NHCA, starting on a CEO-to-CEO basis."

Foster made a dinner engagement with NHCA CEO Mark Hamister, and set out to save the account.

He started by showing Hamister a new perspective on NHCA's business. He explained how NHCA and NovaCare could work together to improve NHCA. "I put together a detailed and extensive presentation. I'd spent some time to learn more about his business than he knew. Using our expertise in our niche of his business, I demonstrated a substantial value-add that other suppliers couldn't match," Foster explains. "Using a proprietary database compiled from NovaCare's 2,100 customers, we could show him on a blind basis how productive his facilities were compared with his competitors and with industry norms. We let him look at his system and showed him data he didn't have. We gave him some new management tools, too: a way to create reasonable objectives for production and productivity, based on site location and size. And we showed him how we could reach those objectives together."

Data, tools, and relationship building have been the glue that have bonded the two companies ever since. They have planned and managed their rehabilitation therapy operations together: They share benchmarks, financial information, and control systems, and they apply innovative outcome-based objectives to assess their joint operational success.

"We work together—vendor and customer—toward a common set of goals and expectations," Foster says. "Everyone is driving toward the same objective. We have mitigated the usual conflicts of customer expectation and vendor expectation; there are fewer opportunities for misunderstanding and miscommunication."

Once again, the distinctions between supplier and customer blur as the partnership grows toward a common goal. NovaCare has assigned a member of its senior staff to managing NHCA's rehab division at NHCA's headquarters. Other NovaCare employees work with planning and budgeting teams at the various NHCA facilities. Employees of both companies hammer out rehabilitation revenue and profit objectives for the upcoming year and seal their plans with a handshake.

"The relationship has remained close at the CEO level, but as time has gone by both Mark Hamister and I have recognized that it is not enough that we have a relationship based on trust and high-quality service," Foster says. "Our counterparts throughout the organization also have to develop those same kinds of relationships."

Like the sign on Foster's wall says, "Relationships Determine Results."

NHCA today is one of NovaCare's biggest customers, providing revenue that has increased from $1 million in 1986 to more than $15 million, including a 30 percent increase in 1995. NHCA, in turn, has enhanced its reputation for delivering better service to its customers, the patients who are the end-users of the therapy the partners provide together. Its financial results reflect patient approval. Revenues for 1995 reached $130 million with $3 million in net income.

"NovaCare has a thorough understanding that I am not the customer," NHCA's Hamister says. "I am merely an intermediary. The customer is the person I am servicing. NovaCare's competitors try to please me all the time. NovaCare does the much harder job of trying to please them and that's what matters in my company. I couldn't care less whether or not suppliers take me out to dinner. They keep me happy only by keeping my customers happy.

"Most of NovaCare's competitors patronize the hell out of the CEOs they do business with," Hamister continues. "If the CEO wants anything done, they do it immediately. But if anyone else in the organization needs something, it's not done at all. NovaCare, frankly, doesn't respond to me any differently than it responds to my unit department heads. And that's the way I want it."

NovaCare's relationship with NHCA is just one of its many carefully nurtured partnerships. NovaCare has worked with other customers to develop a new subacute practice that provides a cost-effective, rehabilitative service. NovaCare has developed new, patented prosthetics in tandem with partners from the managed health-care community, including the insurance companies. But NHCA remains NovaCare's central relationship, according to Timothy Foster, NovaCare's president and COO (and no relation to John Foster). "It's very difficult to imagine either NovaCare or NHCA trying to achieve its strategy for the foreseeable future without the involvement of the other," he says.

Now, after 10 years of steady, mutual growth, the relationship between the two companies is entering another period of turbulence. The rules and economics of the health-care industry are changing. As managed care gains preeminence, health-care buyers look to single-source suppliers reducing their payments for such value-added services as therapist training and database management that aren't related to actual clinical costs. It, therefore, in some cases makes sense for nursing homes to recruit therapists to their own payrolls, for example, rather than contracting for their services with an outside provider like NovaCare.

Foster and Hamister have talked long and hard about how they can meet this challenge. They will have to redefine their strategies and the way their jointly operated therapy business works. Within two years the CEOs expect to have shifted the therapists from NovaCare's payroll to NHCA's. But the two companies will continue to operate their therapy practice together, in partnership. NovaCare will provide training, quality control, clinical evaluations, and recruitment and retention programs.

Neither of the partners knows exactly how the shape of the shared operation will change over the years to come. They'll find the answer together, keeping the focus on results, and meeting patient needs.

SHIFT TO BUSINESS INTEGRATION: THE THIRD MODEL OF PARTNERING

We have seen the persuasive logic that drives companies to move from the first to the second model of partnering. Progressing from joint design to joint operations is a sound way to assure continually improving results. The partners focus the mutual trust that they've been developing since their initial collaboration to search for constant performance gain.

But that same quest for ever-higher performance, in turn, leads some partners to embrace my third model of partnering: business integration. With integration—the most intricate style of partnering—supplier and customer jointly redesign their operating models and business processes, as if they were a single company rather than two distinct entities.

The impetus behind this shift can be as compelling as the impetus behind the shift from model one to model two. Moving from joint operations to business integration is simply the best way for partners to leverage their mutual trust. Their deepening confidence and growing skills let them pursue entirely new ways of doing business together. I could equally well call this third model of partnering "vertical integration without equity." The companies, in practical terms, eliminate the already blurry demarcations between supplier and customer. Each continues to contribute from its strength and expertise, but the form and shape their combined enterprise takes depends on how the newly integrated team best improves the elements of the collaboration. The goal of the partners is to create new value for both of them.

Win Together

Which kind of processes can partners jointly reengineer as they integrate their businesses?

Sales? Forecasting? Purchasing?

Pricing? Inventory? Billing?

Hiring? Training? Cash management?

The answer—for electronics distributor Marshall Industries and contract manufacturer Diagnostic Instrument Corporation—is all of them. When results are all that matter, the only limits to the forms and possibilities of business integration are the limits of the imagination.

Marshall Industries, the nation's fourth largest distributor of electronic components in the U.S., has become customer intimate by necessity. It doesn't sell a unique product; its 10,000 mostly small customers could buy the same supplies from hundreds of other distributors. And it can't compete on price; with so much competition, there is always one who will offer a lower quote. Instead, Marshall sells results: It has led its industry with such innovations as 24-hour service, on-line Internet ordering, and a robotic warehouse that can guarantee 24-hour shipping service.

"We know everybody can sell components," Marshall president and CEO Robert Rodin tells potential customers. "We want to be a virtual distributor allowing customers customized access to our products, services, and information. Any time of the day, from any place on the planet, by any method they choose."

Diagnostic Instrument Corporation, a small player in an equally competitive industry, has become customer intimate, also by necessity. As a high-tech contract manufacturer, it becomes its customer's manufacturing department: Diagnostic takes the designs and specs; it sources, costs, procures, buys, and tests the materials; and finally, it assembles and tests the customer's final product, usually a printed circuit board. With hundreds of contract manufacturers who deliver quality, Diagnostic's ability to compete on speed is a key driver of its success.

"As you try to get closer to your customers you have to get closer to your vendors, aiming for seamless integration among the three of you," Diagnostic's CEO James Hashem says. "The problem is that the typical distributor operates at arm's length, trying to sell each individual product for the most it can, then moving on to the next product and sale."

But Marshall and Diagnostic found a better way that produced dramatically better results for both of them. Three years of integration have helped Diagnostic grow by more than 500 percent, from annual sales of $6 million in 1992 to more than $33 million today. And it has made Diagnostic one of Marshall's significant customers: an $11 million account.

The seed of their integration was planted at a 1992 dinner honoring Marshall as Diagnostic's "Vendor of the Year." A half dozen or so employees from each company sat together into the evening, talking about how far their relationship had progressed during their three years together and where their respective businesses might be going next. For both companies, the problem—and the opportunity—lay in the explosion of subcontracted electronics manufacturing. The potential business for Diagnostic was huge, but with a sales force of only three people, the company was too small to find and capture customers in that growing market. Marshall, in turn, had hundreds of salespeople—25 covering New England alone. Still, subcontracting was creating challenges for Marshall, too. A Marshall salesperson could spend weeks with a prospect's engineering team, specifying parts and assembling information, only to lose the sale when the prospect decided to outsource the work to a contract manufacturer who would choose its own distributor for supply.

That night, the Marshall and Diagnostic people hit on a simple solution. Since Marshall was selling components to customers who often needed assembly work, why not pitch potential customers on the combined capability of their two companies?

But the actual implementation of the joint sales effort was more complicated. Although management at both companies embraced the concept, meeting regularly to push for implementation, the sales teams were slower to sign on. Salespeople, after all, thrive on competition. Learning to collaborate meant a radical change in style as well as a change in commission structure (as we shall see in Chapter 13). As the salespeople talked and trained together—and started to win new business together—they too were eventually convinced that the partnering strategy was the right approach.

The successful joint sales effort brought good feelings to both companies, but it brought a new problem, too. Growing volume at Diagnostic stretched its ability to meet customers' demands. "Our customers demanded very short cycle times from us. Speed to marketplace was their key competitive issue," Hashem explains. "We couldn't do it with traditional purchasing. Sending out for quotes meant it sometimes took us six to eight weeks to answer a customer's questions about availability and cost. But customers need to get their products out quickly, and that means we need to build their prototype quickly.

"Cost is the other major issue," Hashem adds. "Most of the customers we do business with need to lower their costs every six months. So we have to work in a continuous cost-reduction mode, too."

Once again, they met the challenge in partnership, radically reengineering Marshall's way of selling and Diagnostic's materials purchasing.

Diagnostic had always worked with its suppliers in the traditional "pick, pack, and ship" mode: source the inventory, solicit and compare quotes, write the purchase order, sign it, send it, and confirm it. When supplies arrive, log them in. That traditional purchasing system was too slow, too cumbersome, and too costly to meet competitive demands. Delay was inevitable, and overhead was high.

Together the two companies changed their purchasing process. Since most of Diagnostic's orders were already going to Marshall, the partners decided to develop a consigned materials program, making Marshall the Diagnostic vendor of choice.

No longer would they waste time negotiating prices part by part. Instead the two agreed on a uniform pricing formula, which they based on cost and a mutually satisfactory markup.

Management from both companies was eager to try the idea. Both companies first had to persuade the purchasing and sales teams to adopt the new strategy. "The normal buyer is used to going out and getting three prices to make sure to get the lowest," Lori Lucy, Diagnostic's materials manager says. "My argument was that since Marshall was bringing us the customer, Marshall would have every interest in making sure that we are competitive. If we don't win the business, they don't win the business. So it doesn't make sense to spend time and money calling around for better prices."

With prices set, the partners developed a single forecasting system to further speed the process. Each new end customer's monthly forecasts became part of Diagnostic's forecasts, and Diagnostic, in turn, shared its monthly forecasts with Marshall.

With forecasts in place, the two companies established the most visible element of the process redesign: Marshall moved, rent free, into a small space in a Diagnostic building and stocked it with the materials forecasted for use during the coming weeks. They call it the store. Linked to Diagnostic's computer system as a warehouse location and linked to Marshall's main computer in El Monte, California, the store, staffed by a Marshall employee, operates as if it were in a Marshall facility. When Diagnostic employees need parts, the Marshall employee takes care of them.

Operational improvements were immediately impressive. No more FedEx charges for rush shipments. No more delay in answering an end customer's question about, say, delivery dates for extra parts. And, as the partners pushed their redesign, they continued to find new opportunities to improve speed and cut costs.

Purchase orders were the first administrative procedure to go; the partners couldn't justify the overhead costs. Diagnostic had to write them and Marshall had to log them in. They abolished bills for the same reason. Both partners have found it cheaper and faster if Diagnostic runs a list of everything it has taken from the store and forwards it to the accountant for payment.

"Administrative work is where you start saving some money," says Hashem, "and it comes from reducing costs for us both. That means we can reduce costs for our customers and offer better service. It's an absolutely win–win–win situation all the way around."

The partnership even solved Diagnostic's working capital needs. Shut out from additional credit by his bankers, Hashem took his growth plan to Marshall, and the two developed a solution. Marshall extended Diagnostic a line of credit, with payment due in 60 days. Diagnostic, in turn, persuaded its customers to accept a discount in exchange for 10-day payment terms. Having cut the manufacturing cycle time to 4 days and their payment time to 10 days, Diagnostic still had use of the cash for 46 days.

The final change concerned how Marshall's sales staff handles Diagnostic's business. Under the old system, six people had to service the account. With the new consigned materials system in place, one person could easily handle that work. And rather than selling, the salesperson's job now requires sitting with the Diagnostic purchasing group and working to help Diagnostic win the business of its end customer.

"It's a huge dollar savings for them, and it certainly helped us, too," Lori Lucy says. "When we start quoting on jobs and working with customers, Marshall's salesperson is right there. By the time we're actually ready to buy and build the product, we've shaken out the materials problems. We don't have to get on the phone to find something out; somebody lives right here, in plain view. We can go and get anything we need, right on the spot."

Hashem adds, "It cuts overhead for both companies, and gives Marshall a competitive advantage with their other business. Marshall's salesman not only gets to quote every piece of business we do, he gets firsthand information about how the larger market is moving."

This change, too, demanded a major adjustment, Lucy says. "People here worried about putting their salesman inside our purchasing group, where he could see and hear all the details about our business. But I said it didn't matter—we can walk over to his terminal and see everything about his business, too. Who has the time for that? We both have a vested interest in making this work: It's the lowest cost option for both of us. The old mentality—where customers and vendors don't tell each other anything—just doesn't work."

Today the two companies function as one virtual, vertically integrated business, with everyone focused on the same end: better results. Salespeople meet monthly for breakfast to share leads and plan campaigns. Employees from shipping and purchasing departments meet monthly to talk about logistics, looking for still other costs to cut; the MIS staffs meet monthly to improve communications. And senior management meets quarterly, to review the profitability of their thriving partnership and to look for ways to push it forward.

"We need to understand how well we are doing and how we can continue to drive costs down for both of us," Hashem says. "But we have always been clear that neither of us wants to lower margins by taking it out of profits. They decide how much profit they would like to make. We decide how much we would like to make. Everything else is up for grabs. Maybe we are doing something that costs them overhead. How can we change it? Maybe there is something they can change. We're at the point now where we can ask them if they are making money off of us. I don't know of any other two companies where the customer and the vendor sit down to make sure the vendor is making money. If the business isn't profitable for them, in the long term it's not going to work for either of us."

That, right there, is the essence of partnering.

PART III

Cultivate the Human Connections

To this point, I have made the case that customer connections can have a tremendous payoff for both the supplier and the customer. It's almost a situation that is too good to believe. In fact, many managers don't believe it. Indeed, you might be saying to yourself, "All the stories in the first two sections of this book sound wonderful, but aren't the successful customer-intimate firms just lucky to have customers that are willing to let down their guard and share information, share activities, share results?"

What you're asking is how a dyed-in-the-wool manager like yourself should look at these examples. With skepticism? With envy? With hope? I encounter this mixture of thoughts and emotions again and again when I present these stories. Managers yearn to see trust-based customer connections in their firms, yet they have a deep-rooted concern about getting burned. Or they worry about being seen as a "softy" who doesn't truly grasp what "real managers" have always known—that business is essentially an antagonistic affair, that competition and ruthlessness always win.

Given the experiences some suppliers as well as customers have had over the years, skepticism is certainly justified. Put yourself in a customer's shoes. A supplier approaches you and says they want to form a strong bond with you. You immediately wonder what their true motivation might be. Do they want to lull you into some regular patronage? Do they want to turn you into a captive customer so you won't shop around anymore?

Now put yourself in the supplier's shoes. A powerful customer suggests creating a closer working relationship. They might even want to call you a preferred vendor. Are they actually looking to create strong bargaining power by concentrating their business with you (or a few companies they're dealing with)? Will they later try to put the squeeze on you for better terms?

Neither scenario is healthy. What results is an imbalance of power. That is not customer intimacy. True customer intimacy is built on trust, open disclosure, and mutual benefit. These require the supplier and customer to get close to one another, to confide in each other and commit to the process of pursuing mutual benefits. Building a productive customer-intimate relationship is not for the faint of heart.

Fear and suspicion are the major obstacles. The simple suspicion that one party might be trying to gain an advantage is enough to thwart cooperation. It takes courage to overcome fear. It takes trust to accept risk. With that in mind, it's important to take a realistic look at what is required to develop a truly constructive and lasting affiliation. That is the purpose of Part III of this book. The fundamental (and reassuring) lesson is this: Productive connections are very possible, but they must be purposely forged. They do not occur serendipitously.

Thankfully, these connections are not unnatural acts, either. Customer-intimate companies forge productive relationships by pursuing two main tasks: being deliberate in picking partners, and cultivating their ongoing relationships. How to pursue these tasks is the subject of Chapters 8 and 9.

8 | PICK YOUR PARTNERS

Veteran salespeople frequently complain that their company's managers wouldn't recognize a customer if they fell over one. The gibe is often true: Most managers are so caught up in office routines, they never learn who buys their products, why they buy them, or how they use them.

Don't believe it? Try this test: Ask a manager in your company—indeed, ask yourself: "Who are our typical customers? Give me a thumbnail sketch of what they look like, how they view our product, and how they view us." Don't be surprised if the answer is less than illuminating.

Some managers define the typical customer as almost anyone with a few disposable dollars. Others spout data—age, income, marital status, and the like—in lieu of description. But people aren't statistics, and you can't be intimate with numerical averages. Numbers alone can't reflect customer attitudes, behaviors, and experiences, and the company line on those matters is usually so banal as to be meaningless. But until managers really know their customers, how can they possibly pursue effective customer intimacy? How, to start with, can they identify the kind of customers they want to work with, the kind they may have to work with, and the kind they must avoid working with at all costs? For, as we've already seen, an essential part of true—and profitable—intimacy is knowing how to choose the right customer.

There are half a dozen principles that true leaders use to discriminate among prospective customers.

First, they forget about so-called average customers. The old practice of distributing data on a bell-shaped curve and cutting off the extremes simply doesn't apply. Second, they look for customers who focus on the future and are interested in long-term relationships. Third, they look for stretch customers, whose needs and demands require ever-improving performance. Fourth, they assess attitudinal fit and how it would be to work with the prospect. Fifth, they consider the financial outlook of the relationship. And finally, true leaders know when to be cautious: Potential partners that initially appear desirable may turn out to be anything but.

FORGET ABOUT "AVERAGE" CUSTOMERS

To say that someone is a young urban professional between the ages of 25 and 45, with an interest in sports cars, gardening, and gourmet cuisine, is to describe a type or a category. It doesn't describe a person. A major step toward intimacy is to stop thinking in worn categories.

People—changeable and volatile—not stable categories, buy products and services. Classifying along familiar lines blinds us to the heart of the question, which is: What makes these customers potentially good people to connect with?

As I learned from my own experience with the J. Walter Thompson ad agency, there are some companies that many years ago moved beyond the "average customer" mind-set. The firm was intent on knowing precisely at whom to aim its communications. Its explicit philosophy called for each of its ads to touch the hearts and minds of real people, not faceless segments of the population. Copywriters directed their ads to a target person, not a target group, the customary practice. At one point when I was helping to promote a new car model, the agency asked me to write a few pages that would conjure up a target customer. What did that ideal individual look like? What were his tastes in books and movies, political views, dispositions toward dogs and children, feelings about baseball? How would such a person respond to the new car? Why would he desire it? Would he be happy when buying and driving it? Was "he" possibly a "she"?

The writer who directed the ad copy production edited my description until she saw an animated, three-dimensional person standing in front of her: someone she could imagine talking to. You can't have a conversation with a profile that consists only of abstract information and statistics. God is in the details, as Flaubert is credited with having said. And so, we might add, is the customer. No detail that adds flesh and blood to the skeletal frame is irrelevant.

Because of the work they do, ad agencies have always had to be more customer intimate than most other business enterprises. But in all arenas, businesses that have perceived the value of customer intimacy have also rejected gross categorization—segmentation—as an inadequate, unsophisticated tool.

Consumer-marketing companies define segmentation along

several classical lines. Demographic details—age, occupation, sex—have always been leading variables. These marketers segment on the basis of lifestyles by determining what people are most ardent about: Leisure? Self-improvement? Do-it-yourself? Careers?

In industry-to-industry marketing, companies typically segment customers according to size. Others segment according to the specific application of their product or service. Even when both groups use the same product, customers in the chemical industry are considered unlike those in the utility industry. This view arises from the notion that customers with different applications probably have disparate requirements and, as a result, experience different problems.

Geography is another obvious segmentation factor in both the consumer and industry markets. Consider the vast differences between the Northwest and the South, and among city dwellers, suburbanites, and rural residents. Knowing where customers are clustered affects how you organize your sales force, your advertising, and your service organizations.

Still it is hard to accept that although all of this information has value—occasionally great value—it can't help you achieve true intimacy. Customer intimacy is founded on individual, detailed knowledge of a specific person or persons. Conventional market segmentation can't yield such particular knowledge. You need more to forge a productive connection with your customer—a connection that allows you to deliver better results, more individualized and comprehensive solutions.

FOCUS ON THE FUTURE

With segmentation techniques in perspective, you can pursue the second principle: the search for customers who focus on the future, and who are interested in long-term relationships. Customer-intimate companies choose their clientele based more on the future promise they represent than on their current appeal and buying habits.

For would-be customer-intimate companies, an ideal customer is eager to forge an alliance. The customer appreciates what the supplier company has to offer and aims to share the benefits of a cooperative relationship.

Such customers are, obviously, wonderful and, unfortunately, rare. But as I indicated earlier, customer-intimate companies have a longer-term point of view that gives higher value to the quality of relationships with customers than to the quantity. They look for customers who can be trained, developed, groomed, and nurtured into ideal partners.

That approach can lead to some unconventional liaisons. Late in 1995, Compaq, a PC manufacturer, completed a deal to provide Fisher-Price with technology for a recently unveiled line of educational and entertainment products designed for children (ages 3 through 7) and their families. Neither company expects to see a profit anytime soon, but both are thrilled about the future possibilities. Compaq has the technical expertise, and Fisher-Price the toy-marketing know-how, to assure eventual success.

Current customers may be among the best potential long-term partners. But in reviewing their customer lists, suppliers have to make important distinctions. Many in the business world advocate assessing the lifetime value of each customer: the amount of business a customer will generate over the duration of their relationship. That's fine, as an exercise, but it assumes that what customers buy today indicates how much they will buy tomorrow. But why miss out on the potential to develop more business with a particular customer? By getting closer to a customer, you can better understand that customer's needs and find new ways to cater to those needs, enhance your relationship, and create new business opportunities.

SEEK "STRETCH" CUSTOMERS

The best customer-intimate companies go one step further. When they look for prospects that are potentially ideal partners, they keep an eye out for candidates that will challenge them. I call such a customer a stretch customer: It stretches its suppliers to the limit and, in so doing, makes them stronger.

Clearly, that kind of relationship can tax the supplier. But the rewards are commensurate. Not only does the successfully stretched supplier find better ways to deal with its regular customers, but, as a result of growing beyond the competitive herd, it also ends up attracting other, bigger, and even more strategic customers. Customer-intimate companies view their stretch customers as ideal protection from complacency. Those customers force their suppliers to learn, grow, and provide value year after year.

Silicon Graphics, Inc., a leading manufacturer of high-performance visual computing systems, identifies a group of its end users as "lighthouse" customers. This select group works with the company in the development and implementation of its products. Silicon Graphics sets a limit on the number of its lighthouse customers in order to stay focused on its primary mission—providing end users with technologies that allow them to differentiate in their markets.

SIZE UP THE ATTITUDINAL FIT

Attitudinal fit calls for both parties to share a similar mind-set, and an unwavering commitment to the success of their partnership. Both sides must exhibit patience and tolerance—plain words that lead to hard deeds. Moreover, the cultures of customer and supplier must be compatible. Some companies forgo an opportunity if the prospect doesn't embrace a philosophy of collaboration.

The importance of attitudinal fit sometimes supersedes even the technical competencies of a potential partner. In 1986, according to *Fortune* magazine, Honda chose Donnelly Corp. of Michigan to make the exterior mirrors for its U.S.-manufactured cars. Donnelly had supplied Honda with interior mirrors but had never before made exterior mirrors. Honda could have chosen another vendor with a documented track record, but because Donnelly's culture and values matched its own, Honda chose instead to develop a small reengineering program that prepared Donnelly for the new task. In return, Donnelly built a new plant dedicated to manufacturing exterior mirrors. Donnelly also benefited by developing a new product line it can sell to other carmakers.

Honda had an advantage of already knowing Donnelly's culture. But when you deliberate over new recruits, how can you tell which companies will cultivate a philosophy that works with yours? Caliber Logistics, Inc., uses several tests.

Openness is the first. The potential customer must be open about cost structures and strategies. If that openness is not present from the start, it's unlikely ever to develop. Openness is especially important to Caliber Logistics, whose people work very closely— almost within—the customer's organization. If the customer is not forthcoming, the Caliber Logistics representative would be operating in the dark.

Even in circumstances where a few attitudinal incongruencies linger, some friction is inevitable when a supplier and customer first work intimately together—there must be one or more people in the customer's organization who champion the idea of customer intimacy. A supplier has to determine whether the potential partner has influential people in positions to promote the concept.

In Caliber Logistics' view, a company that's serious about customer intimacy will not only have convinced itself of the value of such a relationship, but will have also assembled a team that supports a smooth interface for the relationship. People from sales, marketing, legal, financial, and information systems—or some combination of them—should be in communication from the start.

Other cultural criteria can help indicate whether a target company has the right attitudinal fit. Caliber Logistics wants to be challenged, and its experience has shown that the young are more likely to be challengers. Caliber Logistics therefore takes the age factor into account. "We love a young, entrepreneurial company," says Tom Escott, the vice president of sales and marketing at Caliber Logistics. "Those are the kinds of companies that we align with very well. Fast moving, out-of-the-box thinking."

Customer intimacy is a new practice, an ongoing experiment. Fluidity and flexibility are essential features on both sides. Caliber Logistics may prefer to deal with younger companies because youth is usually associated with flexibility, openness, and a taste for fresh ideas. It's important to realize, however, that what counts here is not age but attitude. The young can be obstinate and cavalier, while some mature companies have learned the value of give-and-take.

CONSIDER THE FINANCIAL OUTLOOK

When you can mesh operations and attitudes with minimal gear grinding, it's time to talk money. That brings us to the next qualification for the best potential customers: financial fit.

When a supplier and its customer reach a quid pro quo arrangement, they establish a financial fit. That means the supplier is willing to share some of the customer's risk in return for a portion of the customer's profits derived from the supplier's goods or services. A customer-intimate company might go so far as to say, "I am willing to sacrifice some of my fees, lower my prices, and give you a break right now. But later, I want to share in the upside."

That approach is motivationally terrific all around. The supplier delivers a message of confidence to the customer. The supplier's investment can take several forms. Several years ago, when Caliber Logistics was still Roadway Logistics Systems (ROLS), it performed electronic-data-interchange applications for Compaq that, from the start, were clearly not going to be profitable transactions for ROLS. It did the work with high expectations of gaining advantage over the long term. On the face of it, it seems like standard practice. The difference in this case, however, was that ROLS used the opportunity not just to demonstrate its value to Compaq but also to inaugurate an intimate relationship. It made sure Compaq got a real feel for who ROLS was. It worked. Compaq is now a major account.

ROLS played a different investment game with Sun Microsystems. Even after it lost a bid, ROLS stayed in touch with Sun, keeping Sun apprised of its new services and systems. ROLS was deliberately building a relationship. ROLS' actions conveyed the message: "We want to work with you. We're good, and we're willing to wait. When you're ready, we'll be here." Eighteen months later, Sun was ready and ROLS was there.

A customer's willingness to share profits is especially important when the supplier makes demonstrable contributions to its client's success. The painter who paints the walls of a butcher shop cannot claim much share in the owner's success, but the painter who produces an attractive sign that lures customers merits a thicker slice.

Customer-intimate companies have to be careful about how they design their deals, however. Take the case of Leo Burnett, the ad agency that created the Marlboro Man. As one of the most successful images in the history of advertising, there can be little doubt that the success of the cigarette brand itself is closely linked to the power of that image. It was a case of shared triumph all around, but not shared rewards. Leo Burnett earned nothing beyond its standard commissions. Back in the 1960s, ad agencies expected no more. Today, however, an agency might well seek to establish intimacy by approaching the customer with a different proposition: "Rather than paying us a straight fee or commission, why don't we design a tie-in with the gains you derive from the campaign? For example, if you realize an X percent gain in market share, then you will increase our fees by five percent. If the brand becomes really successful, we'll tie additional fees to the number of units you sell, or increases in your market share over a specific period of time."

More and more customer-intimate companies pursue such arrangements. Although they're riskier for the supplier, they can also lead to greater payoffs. The customer, who might think he's giving up a little more profit than he'd like, should give serious consideration to such an offer: The supplier has dramatically enhanced motivation to make a sustainable, long-term success out of its work. Take the relationship between Nypro Inc., the plastic-injection company, and Verbatim, the floppy-disk maker. To raise its production quality to world-class levels, Verbatim had to retool. But it was strapped for cash. Nypro, which wanted to spread its overhead across more volume production, decided to fund Verbatim's improvements. In return, Verbatim's increased business with Nypro not only helped Nypro spread costs but also added to its high-volume sales.

Even if a customer-intimate supplier's investment in a customer doesn't yield a profitable relationship (some relationships do fail), the supplier can still derive benefit. The supplier will learn from each relationship, particularly from the stretch customers. Not only do stretch customers force a supplier to reach and to grow, they also prepare the supplier for other stretch customers down the line.

Establishing whether supplier and customer can profitably share risk and reward is the real test of a financial fit. In Chapter 12, we'll discuss the economics of intimacy in greater detail.

WATCH FOR RED FLAGS

It's vital to recognize your ideal customers. It's also smart to recognize the red flags that signal an apparently appealing prospect that could mean trouble.

Customer-intimate companies are especially leery of three types of customers. The first are those with a history of one-time buying. Such customers use the market in standard fashion, shopping around to obtain the best deal. They have no record of standing by one or a few of their suppliers. They chase short-term gains rather than the benefits of a close, lasting connection with a particular company.

One red flag that indicates a one-shot dealer is a request for proposal (RFP) mailed indiscriminately to anyone appearing in the business directory. RFPs are common practice in industrial fields. A purchasing department drafts a concise set of specifications for a product or service. It distributes an RFP to a variety of suppliers to obtain the best proposal. Seasoned customer-intimate companies respond to RFPs that truly play to their strengths. If the RFP reveals an inveterate player-of-the-field, they avoid them.

The self-sufficient, control-obsessed customers constitute a second troublesome category. Those customers don't want much bridge-building, partnering, or coaching. They're do-it-yourselfers. Intimacy makes them nervous. Their managers feel the need to control everything in their business, and, consequently, they strive to control everything in their suppliers' businesses as well. They keep their suppliers on constant notice. They don't want anyone getting too relaxed because they're convinced they have to be aggressive to exact the best deal. In addition to being aggravating, those customers have no interest in broader solutions. They don't value the full range of what customer intimacy has to offer. This doesn't make them unsuccessful in their own terms, but it always makes them incompatible with your terms.

The last category of prospects not worth pursuing are those who have no patience. They won't take the time to bring a longer-term relationship to fruition. Those customers want answers right away. They want a product yesterday. They're not inclined to invest time to find what ultimately might be a better solution. The red flag they raise is their insistence on a quick fix. They sulk when they have to wait. Such people can't imagine that long-term intimacy might benefit their businesses.

Tom Escott, vice president of sales and marketing for Caliber Logistics, Inc., is always on the lookout for signs of impatience. Caliber Logistics has successfully dealt with nearly every aspect of customer intimacy. But most impressive is Caliber Logistics' incredible willingness to be selective about its customers. Caliber Logistics will not entertain a relationship with a prospect that hasn't independently recognized that it must outsource logistics because it isn't among its core competencies. "The first thing we look for is a company that's done this internal work," Escott says. Otherwise, he says, Caliber Logistics is in for "a big education process and a convincing process."

TRIAGE: LET GO OF MEDIOCRE CUSTOMERS

But, you may well ask, how can I afford to invest aggressively in the best future customers if I'm spending my resources on current, less-than-satisfactory customers?

Good question. The past decade has seen a major development in the corporate world: supplier rationalization. Xerox, for example, expended untold effort monitoring and managing more than 3,000 suppliers. Today, after scrutinizing each relationship, Xerox has decimated that number. Many companies conducted similar rationalizations. In the end they have fewer but more complete relationships that yield many of the benefits that derive from strong supplier-customer connections.

The irony is that suppliers are not doing the same thing with their customers. And why not? A supplier with too many customers suffers the same headaches and inefficiencies as a customer with too many suppliers. Suppliers who want to develop customer–intimate relationships must reduce the number of their customers, or they'll never be able to spend the time and effort needed to establish a rewarding connection with any of them. Suppliers, in other words, have to go through a process of triage.

In customer triage, suppliers must make two hard decisions. The first: which clients to serve? The second concerns the type and depth of relationship it wants to establish with its remaining customers. Nypro's experience to the contrary, it's not always the case that the biggest customers repay the greatest efforts of collaboration. Time and time again, I've seen suppliers diligently cater to major corporations, and gain little or nothing for their trouble. This is tough to recognize and even tougher to act upon. What do you do if you determine you should divest yourself of one of your biggest customers? There are two options.

One action is to swap customers. Try to find another large prospect that has hesitated to deal with you while you work with its competitor. Approach the prospect gingerly and ask what might happen should you disengage yourself from the rival. Would it entertain working with you? If you can move from the undesirable customer to the more attractive replacement, you will clearly be better off, and the new customer will benefit greatly by now having you in its camp.

The second way to leave an undesirable customer calls for gradual disengagement. Suddenly dropping a customer can damage your business and your reputation. At Caliber Logistics, they call this tactic "unselling."

Plastics maker Nypro reduced its customer base from 800 to 80. CEO Gordon Lankton deliberately clipped ties with numerous small customers so Nypro could develop greater sales volumes with a smaller number of large companies. Today, 40 customers or so bring in $1 million or more per year, and another 40 are approaching that mark. Nypro has formed successful partnerships with many of those customers. A number of them consult Nypro in the design of new products. As Lankton is the first to acknowledge, Nypro could never have sustained similarly valuable partnerships with 800 customers.

When Nypro let go of so many customers, it carefully avoided burning its bridges. "We explained to those customers what our new focus was and that they could get better service from a different type of injection molder," says Randall S. Barko, Nypro's vice president of sales and marketing. Nypro went to the trouble of helping them to find new suppliers. Nypro's solicitude paid off. "We have had several of those customers, who revitalized a year or two later with bigger programs, come back and ask if it would make sense for us to get together again," Barko says.

Another harder-to-recognize outcome of triage is worth pursuing: Triage can require some case study, and, in the course of your review, you might find that some of your seemingly undesirable customers actually warrant additional attention.

THE FINAL PARTNERS

In summary, every intimate relationship involves some degree of understanding and risk. Customer intimacy means sharing: sharing knowledge, sharing risk, and sharing profit. To decide which customers are worth the effort, customer-intimate companies objectively—without relying on predetermined categories—define who their target customers are. They look for customers with whom they can build long-term relationships, even those who will stretch their capabilities. They also know when to be cautious about a seemingly good prospect.

As it makes its final choices about its most desirable customers, a supplier tests its finalists to see which provide the best attitudinal, operational, and financial fit. Once it identifies the hottest prospects, the company makes the hard choice to divest itself of some current customers so it can focus its time and energy on those with even greater potential.

Those tasks completed, the real fun begins: Engaging those promising partners.

9 | GET CONNECTED

It doesn't come naturally for suppliers or buyers to establish customer-intimate connections of the kind I described in the chapters on tailoring, coaching, and partnering. Such connections are different in several important respects from traditional dealings or one-time transactions.

That was evident in 1985, when, after a long history of working at arm's length, Procter & Gamble forged a customer-intimate relationship with Wal-Mart, then as now its largest customer. (Wal-Mart's share of P&G's business is currently about 13 percent.) The purpose was to drive excess costs out of the supply chain.

For one thing, such a connection required a heightened level of mutual trust—not a natural trait for managers who had been dealing with each other from afar, often in a "we win–you lose" mode. Lou Pritchett, at the time P&G's vice president of sales, and Wal-Mart founder Sam Walton started off the process of trust-building with a boat trip down the South Fork River in Arkansas—quite a departure from the prior impersonal contacts between the two firms. Intrigued by what might come from establishing a closer relationship, they convened their top officers to become personally acquainted. Further discussion and soul-searching led these executives to form a team of 12 people—representing sales, marketing, and information systems of the two companies—chartered to come up with new ways to do business and cut inefficiencies.

The next challenge was defining the scope of the companies' mutual involvement. One of the first areas the two firms looked at was Wal-Mart's undesirably high inventory levels. P&G said they could help—by using a computerized inventory replenishment model to figure the optimal pattern for Wal-Mart to place orders—initially for one product line, Pampers diapers. P&G's modelers pored over Wal-Mart's warehouse inventory information and purchase order data, and then produced a suggested purchase order for Wal-Mart's approval on a daily basis. After a few weeks, Wal-Mart asked to be removed from that approval loop—after all, why create more work than necessary.

Over time, the scope of involvement expanded. Other products and items were included in this automated replenishment process, and P&G started to advise Wal-Mart on moving inventory between warehouses and stores, and from warehouse to warehouse. P&G in effect became Wal-Mart's order management and logistics coach. Working together called for a break from the practice they had grown up with: fulfillment of discrete, well-defined orders. The new emphasis was on reshaping their day-to-day interactions: Customer intimacy put a premium on building a strong interface between closely cooperating supplier and customer.

The outcome: Wal-Mart was able to reduce its out-of-stock situations. P&G's on-time delivery improved to 99.6 percent from 94 percent, with a lot of related savings for both supplier and customer. Wal-Mart's sales (and hence P&G's sales) went up because shelf space was now used to sell, not as a buffer to store inventory. A doubling of Pampers' inventory turns made available shelf space for other P&G products, lots of sales calls were eliminated, and order management and logistics staff at both firms were freed up to deal with more pressing concerns.

As the travails of these two companies illustrate, getting connected calls for building trust, managing the scope of involvement, and strengthening the interface so supplier and customer evolve to the point where working and winning together become second nature. Those are the themes we'll discuss in this chapter.

ESTABLISH TRUST

With customer intimacy, the fates of suppliers and customers are increasingly intertwined, and interdependence, rather than independence, is the new watchword. It's common for prospective customers to feel uneasy or even apprehensive about a supplier's quest for a closer connection. Many prospects are tentative, taking a wait-and-see attitude. When a supplier approaches such potential customers with notions of commitment to results and sharing confidences, they may recoil. Their unfamiliarity with those precepts of the customer-intimate discipline and their lack of prior experience with suppliers who want to work cooperatively are two hurdles. The uncertainties that obscure the payoff, and their anxiety about close relationships can be showstoppers.

Prospective customers—and their suppliers—need to prepare themselves emotionally for the shift to intimacy. In every successful customer-intimate company I've come across, such emotional preparation involves a process of building respect and gaining mutual confidence.

Without respect for and confidence in each other, the connection is doomed to falter. No customer who views the supplier as a second-class citizen will be truly open to being coached, to working side by side.

Caliber Logistics' Bill Jones, vice president of transportation and business development, considers respect the starting point of trust. "We earn more and more trust through each individual success, but you can't get anywhere without mutual respect. If you have customers looking at you as a nonstrategic supplier, it creates suspicion and bad feelings all around. Morale drops, productivity drops, everyone loses."

To build respect, customer intimacy pros invariably demonstrate genuine care for the customer. As a colleague of mine says, "Customers want to know how much you care before they care about how much you know." Unless suppliers evidence empathy, customers won't disclose what's really on their mind: their key issues, hopes, fears, or true difficulties.

Prudent customer-intimate suppliers are astute observers of their customers' state of mind and how they feel about suppliers. They ask themselves such questions as

➤ What are the customers' biggest concerns about the issues that face them? About suppliers in general? About us?

➤ What has the customer done so far to deal with the issue? Has it had any success? Or is it coming to this relationship fresh from failure? Is there any scar tissue to watch out for?

➤ If the customer has experienced recent setbacks, does it know the causes? And can it coherently communicate the reasons for any successes?

➤ Who are our competitors in the field? Has the customer already dealt with any of them? If so, with what results? What is our differentiating advantage vis-à-vis those competitors?

The answers to those questions give the supplier insight in the process of gaining the prospect's confidence. Companies that aren't customer intimate typically establish their credentials with consistency of performance: Everyone, for example, knows what to expect from McDonald's and Federal Express. Other companies rely on a strong brand name: Even with evidence that other brands work well, many people select a Sony product, or Panasonic's, because they are the brands they have learned to trust. Important as those approaches are, their relevance pales in customer-intimate companies. Those suppliers' nonstandard offerings are harder to judge, and they rely more on the credibility of personal referrals than on brand building.

Before they feel confidence in the supplier, customers want to know what they are betting on, and the supplier needs to be aware of this. Is the customer placing his bet on your technology? Or on you as a frontline person, an executive who has made him promises? Or on your company's staying power? Or on its financial resources and strength? Or its product family? Supplier and customer must share an understanding of risk and bet: If they don't, they're not playing the same game.

The customer-intimate enterprise builds its customer's confidence by demonstrating it knows what it's doing. Providing evidence it's successful in situations similar to those its prospect faces is an effective way to enhance its status. And it doesn't hurt to demonstrate how its approach differs from the familiar, traditional arm's-length relationships. It's important for the supplier to know the customer's business. And, in order to nurture mutual understanding and trust, the customer ought to understand the supplier's business, too. But ultimately, the coveted state of full customer trust is unattainable until the supplier delivers on the expectations it has set and the commitments it has made. Reaching that state takes time. As Nypro's Gordon Lankton says, "It can take two or three years for us to trust each other fully."

Forging radically new relationships requires innovative methodology. Some companies have organized Outward Bound–like camping experiences that stretch their own people's and their customers' perspective on working together and trusting each other. While such expeditions might, at first glance, appear misguided, they've proven valuable. People who together brave the Arizona desert, explore the forests of Maine, learn to sail, or hike through five feet of snow, connect in ways that are more profound than ordinary social situations allow. The mutual respect and empathy such outings inspire become immutable parts of the customer-supplier relationship.

In Chapter 6, we saw how Quad/Graphics, the Wisconsin-based printing company, uses CAMP/Quad to show its customers how they can work most effectively with Quad. But the camp and other vendor–customer outings promote one-on-one bonding.

Pamela Rostagno, a Quad service manager, describes the value of a wet and wild whitewater rafting trip. "People are out of their element, out of their offices, away from their jobs. They spend 48 hours together, learning about one another, building trust. Later, if there is a problem or crisis in the course of business, their personal relationships have a solid grounding. I think that it's a little harder to scream at somebody and fly off the handle when you've shared an experience like rafting that is filled with emotional extremes and exhilaration. You all feel equally vulnerable when you're headed for the rocks. And there's no time to hide it."

Back on the job, people apply the problem-solving lessons they learn at such camps and weekend excursions. When customer and supplier have struggled to forage for dinner on the forest floor or to steer the raft from dangerous rapids, their once-insurmountable problems take more manageable forms.

SCOPE THE CONNECTION

When I make a routine, well-defined purchase of, say, a suit off the rack, I know exactly what I'm getting. Things are murkier when I place a special order for a tailor-made suit. I don't quite know how it will work out until it's ready. Customers often view the offerings of customer-intimate companies with similar apprehension. As they establish a foundation of trust, therefore, supplier and customer need also to clarify exactly what the customer is buying and what will be the exact scope of their connection.

I've found that intimate connections are far more productive when they start with the right issue: an issue with good enough substance to attract the customer's serious attention and interest and the potential to grow over time. What doesn't work well is to jam your foot in the door by initially tackling a minor issue in the hopes of a later expanding role. The problem with a low-key approach is that it limits the supplier's opportunity to position itself as a purveyor of comprehensive solutions rather than a provider of partial, small answers. Later, that supplier may have to fight an uphill battle to establish its true credentials and potential.

When it zeros in on a meaty challenge, a smart supplier makes sure it is not only capable of handling it, but will actually excel at handling it. As it illuminates the customer's problems, it spotlights its own abilities and personal bests.

To determine the scope of involvement, suppliers contemplate:

➤ What is the exact nature of the customer's problem and the specific goals he would like to achieve?

➤ How does the customer understand and define his problems and goals? Is there any disparity between the customer's own understanding and the way he presents it?

➤ Why is this a problem now? Has this issue been a long time coming or is it something sudden? What is the urgency factor?

➤ Does the problem play to our strength or are others better qualified to deal with it? Is this a moment of opportunity or time for triage?

➤ Last and most important, do the customer's needs and nature point him inevitably in the direction of customer intimacy, or is another solution more appropriate?

In a nutshell, the customer-intimate company must have room to apply its commercial imagination and work its way up the customer's hierarchy of needs: Starting with a narrow definition can constrict opportunities for the creative, effective solutions that are oxygen to customer intimacy.

Still, the supplier should not saddle itself with unrealistically high expectations that are doomed from the start. There are two caveats to keep in mind: Don't overstretch, and don't move too fast.

You overstretch if your customer's expectations exceed your abilities. It's a sure way to turn the relationship sour. Your goal is to set up viable, productive relationships, not disappointment-strewn disasters.

Persistence was the key to Airborne Express's profit-winning relationship with Nike, Inc. As Bruce Grout, vice president and general manager of Airborne's Pacific Area remembers it, success came from "putting one foot in front of the other, like working your way through a maze."

Airborne began by proposing to establish a computer-based communication link with Nike. According to Grout, this system gave Nike's shipping process "total visibility." It could follow every step, from the minute Airborne received a shipment to the minute it delivered the goods to their final destination. "Nike had complete understanding of what the time parameters were. This gave them realistic expectations of delivery time. It helped them understand our end of things and boosted confidence."

By not promising more than it could do, Airborne earned Nike's confidence and respect. But the relationship was not so narrowly defined that it eliminated room for growth. With one significant success under way, it was only natural for Airborne to expand Nike's service to include Singapore and, later, the demanding and lucrative shipments between Asia and Europe.

Nike expected neither too much nor too little of Airborne, and, as a result, they have an expanding partnership that has enhanced the productivity and profits of both companies.

The second caveat I mentioned concerns moving too fast. Just as you can't reduce a cake's baking time by raising the oven temperature, you need to allow time for customer connections to mature. Too often, I've observed companies not only trying to speed the sales process, but also trying to establish an aggressive expansion and recasting of the customer's operations that is far beyond what the customer wants.

When you're establishing a connection with a prospect, and things are going well—trust is being established, the scope of engagement is getting clarified—it's natural to want to accelerate the process and get down to business. Natural or not, excessive speed is a major pitfall. Having an answer to a customer's problem is so exhilarating, it's tempting to act before you really understand the problem.

But, you say, you once dealt with an identical situation. Can't you draw on your experience to fill in blanks and formulate a solution? No, you can't. Drawing on experience is an essential aspect of customer intimacy. As we pointed out in the last chapter it gives the supplier a distinct advantage. But no two situations are exactly alike, and you can't factor in your past experience until you understand the present customer inside and out. Rushing through a problem won't foster that understanding.

Don't forget, you are forging a relationship. You want the customer to travel at your speed. Customers may never have dealt with the issues you're raising, and when they find themselves in unfamiliar territory, instinct will tell them to move slowly. Allow them time to catch up. Have your customer review his or her concerns slowly and diligently, articulating problem areas and difficult processes. Gradually, awareness will grow—for customer and supplier alike. When people hear each other out, learn together, and arrive at conclusions at the same moment, they establish a gratifying bond. It's impossible to experience that mutual satisfaction when one party presses another to move faster.

STRENGTHEN THE INTERFACE

Nowhere are intimate connections more visible than in the ongoing contact between supplier and customer. Their interface is the locus of activity, the hub from which smooth interactions radiate. That interface can't rely on a single salesperson's staying in touch with a single buyer. Several people at the supplier's company can communicate with their appropriate counterparts in the buying organization. In a customer-intimate interface, cooperation often occurs at several levels. Proper preparation always pays off handsomely. The questions to consider when building an interface are those an astute sociologist or politician would ponder:

➤ Does the customer have experience dealing cooperatively with outside suppliers or consultants? If so, how well have those dealings gone?

➤ What are the customer's strengths and weaknesses? Do they dovetail nicely with ours?

➤ Which key people in the customer's organization will determine the fate of our attempts to promote customer intimacy? Who are the champions? Who are the potential saboteurs?

➤ What kind of relationship do your supporters have? Are they well-aligned with each other and within the company's organizational system? What stake does each of them have in the customer–intimacy issue?

The linchpin of every close alliance is a senior decision-maker in the buyer's organization, who is involved in and committed to the customer-intimate relationship. His or her clout will provide the reassuring and driving force to make the connection work.

Bill Jones, vice president of transportation and business development for Caliber Logistics, Inc., considers this a key point: "We need to have a sponsor within the customer's organization, someone who has the authority to mandate change. The sponsor gets out the message that the company is going to support the operation and won't tolerate sabotage or let it deteriorate."

This is not to say that the connection rests on only one such person. Nypro's Gordon Lankton has a simple rule: For every million dollars of business, he wants Nypro people in contact with five of the customer's employees. Getting qualified staff involved in implementing the proposed solutions is critical. Experience-hardened customer–intimate companies make sure that their people get acquainted with the appropriate customer teams right from the start. In addition to creating the required operational environment, it signals a necessary seriousness of intent.

It's often the case in customer-intimate relationships that members of one organization also work well in the other. When Caliber Logistics, for example, handles such large and complex accounts as GM and Dell, it identifies a person from Caliber Logistics who matches the client's ideal of a logistics vice president, and it places him or her within the client's organization. By virtue of the position he or she occupies, that on-site vice president of logistics is in a perfect position to scout possibilities for a greater and more mutually profitable relationship.

Once the person is in place, a constructive and regular flow of communication becomes an imperative source of strength. One condition of success is absolute specificity about each party's role and contributions. You must establish clarity of purpose and clarity of expectation from the start. But you must also check continually to be sure that expectations don't deviate.

When Caliber Logistics presents its final pricing to a customer, the details and goals are clear to everyone involved: both in the customer's company and within Caliber Logistics itself. The project-preparation process involves Caliber Logistics officers in information systems, industrial engineering, accounting, marketing and sales, and operations. No one is left in the dark. The teams that designed and will implement the proposal present it to the customer.

According to Robert Nicholson, Caliber Logistics' regional vice president of sales and marketing, the sale itself does not define success. "Success is implementing a project that adds value to the customer's company. And that means that everyone involved has to understand and embrace the terms of what that added value truly is. We all have to embrace the actual partnership we're forming, not some fantasy partnership that doesn't exist."

Discussion of difficult issues also strengthens the interface. Seasoned customer-intimate companies inform customers during the earliest stages of the contact—and throughout their relationship—

that they're not meek and won't hesitate to discuss the most formidable and stubborn obstacles. And they let them know that their customers expect them to do the same. The sooner everyone acknowledges a problem and discusses it, the sooner it can be solved.

Let's say that, for one reason or another, the customer no longer enjoys the high level of economic benefit to which it became accustomed. The numbers might even suggest finding another supplier. A wide-awake supplier would not be caught off-guard by such a development. The savvy supplier would have discussed it with its customer and attempted to build flexibility into their contract. The key is maintaining an open, honest exchange of information.

In the long run, enduring and surviving the down times together helps to create greater trust. That was Airborne's experience when it opened Nike's pick-and-pack operation in Singapore. Airborne took delivery of goods from all over Asia, warehoused them, and, after receiving electronic information from Nike, delivered the goods and supplied Nike with proof of delivery. The problem was that volume ran at about 20 times the magnitude Airborne had anticipated, based on information from Nike. Foul-ups were rampant. Or, as Carl K. Davis, director of international trade for Nike, puts it: "Everything went totally to hell." The two sides agreed that it was "hell," differing only in their assessment of its dimensions.

The two companies had, however, built their relationship on frank communication and honest expectations that allowed for admissions of error and chances to redress problems. Instead of blowing up, Davis took a problem-solving stance: "I told Airborne the problem may be partly my fault, partly theirs, but I was getting my butt chewed out something fierce. We had to see if we could fix this thing. Right away, they were here for us."

In the words of Airborne's Bruce Grout, "We told Nike right from the start we'd be honest. We said, 'Hey, we made a mistake. You threw us more than what you said you would, and we didn't handle it well. But we do have a plan.' Their comeback was, 'We understand. Can you promise you'll make this work?' We said, 'Yes.' And they rode with us."

In fact, they rode together. Both sides had work to do: Nike had to take responsibility for ensuring that their field sales force submitted accurate projections, working with Airborne to develop a new scheduling system. Airborne then executed the revised plan.

Davis acknowledges that "to do business with Nike from a service-provider's point of view is tough. We make a lot of demands on our people. We make a lot of demands on ourselves. We are number one in the world, and we didn't get there by not charging hard. We make the same demands on the service providers who do business with us. And we put those cards right on the table at the very beginning of the relationship."

If open communication and flexibility had not been built into the partnership, Airborne would have stumbled through the dark, unable to acknowledge its difficulties, afraid to ask for assistance. Nike would have abandoned a working relationship that—with some adjustments and improvements—turned out to be highly successful.

COMMUNICATE, COMMUNICATE, COMMUNICATE

In customer-intimate connections, communication can occur in unexpected forms. Customer councils are an example of how supplier and customers can share honest, constructive feedback. A customer-council meeting lets managers from several client organizations meet with their supplier to share experiences and ideas for improving their connection. In every such meeting I've attended, I've noted the eye-opening frankness and empathy both the supplier and the customers demonstrate.

I recently attended one such session hosted by Staples National Advantage. About a dozen vocal customers created an atmosphere that reminded me of an elite club, with experts vying to share their experiences. I'm convinced everyone left feeling nourished.

Whether such exchanges occur routinely or during special council sessions, open communication at every level of the interface has the additional benefit of reinforcing the trust-building process. Robert Rodin, president and CEO of Marshall Industries, is very direct with his customers: If he's not already on the line, he picks up his own phone to answer incoming calls. Customers are startled the first time, but their surprise quickly gives way to delight. "It's a simple way to stay in touch with randomly chosen customers," says Rodin. "All my management does this as a matter of policy."

Northwestern Mutual Life Insurance takes a more complex approach to demonstrating its concern for customers. That company was among the first to adopt a mission statement—in 1888. Jim Ericson, president and CEO, describes its mission as follows: "Everything that we do—every decision we make—is based on what we think is good both for our customers and our owners." Northwestern is a mutual company, so customers are owners. The company's 7,200 sales agents learn to be skilled listeners, to be contemplative, and never to rush a sale. "I know most people think of insurance agents as people who talk a lot," says Ericson. "But at Northwestern, we focus on drawing customers out." The company stresses warmth, face-to-face communication, and the personal touch.

As Robert E. Carlson, executive vice president, marketing, explains: "A good insurance agent should know more about an individual and/or family than any other professional. A lawyer knows a piece of the story, medical people know a piece, the church yet another piece. We make sure our agents know all the pieces."

Northwestern Mutual Life takes an unusual approach to open communications. Every year, Northwestern asks five policyholders—all seasoned executives—to spend several days visiting its company offices. It encourages them to nose around any areas they choose, to inspect and audit whatever they want. This group of customers—the Policy Owner Examining Committee—writes a report to all policy holders, the CEO, and the board of trustees. No holds barred. To top off this remarkable openness, Northwestern publishes the committee's findings in its annual report.

In the words of Jim Ericson, "The committee members set their own agenda. They talk with company lawyers, auditors, the union—basically, anyone they want to talk to. We couldn't throw the doors open any wider. It's a tremendous way to learn what your customers are really concerned about, what they're thinking. And it's our way of letting them know we have nothing to hide."

USE YOUR CONNECTIONS

In closing, let me revisit P&G and Wal-Mart. After P&G figured out how to boost Wal-Mart's performance, it realized that other customers would benefit from similar arrangements. The next customer it approached was Toys "R" Us, which expressed a somewhat different need—replenish our diapers at the store level, not at a warehouse. P&G customized its solution to accommodate that situation, and has since pursued intimate connections with a host of other major customers.

Likewise, Wal-Mart has learned from its connection with P&G and has ever since been replicating it with selected suppliers. A few years back, it went so far as to invite 500 suppliers to its Bentonville, Arkansas, offices to brief them on what it calls extended partnership arrangements.

What in the mid-1980s had been regarded, in the words of P&G I/S manager Michael Graen, as "extraordinary requests from a logistics standpoint," had by the mid-1990s become the standard way of doing business for both Wal-Mart and P&G.

It puts new meaning in the words "getting connected."

PART IV

Commit the Corporation

The customer-intimate companies whose stories I've been telling are a distinct breed of America's winning corporations. Most notably, as we saw in Parts II and III, they are extraordinarily committed to their customers' results. Their dedication to another's flourishing is as plain as day. You see it in the many different ways in which these companies strive to serve their markets, in the persistence and resourcefulness with which they maintain close connections with selected customers, and in their dedication to finding better and better solutions to customers' problems.

When you look at those enterprises from the inside, as we'll be doing in this section, you'll observe other distinctive traits they all share. First, to provide individualized solutions, the customer-intimate firm operates more like a collection of niche businesses than like a monolith. Second, its closeness to the customer is mirrored internally in its open, flexible, cooperative processes and operations. And third, more than most other companies, a customer-intimate company is truly knowledge-hungry—forever striving to get smarter about its markets, its customers, its customers' competitors, and the state of its art. If one word could sum up the stand-out qualities of customer-intimate companies, that word would be "agility"—as in, "operational agility." And if one stand-out principle could be said to guide their marketplace behavior, it would be to commit—as in, commit the whole company.

None of those characteristics or operating principles come about by chance. They all require doing several things right. If you take a deeper look inside customer-intimate suppliers, you'll see that, first, everything emanates from the right culture—a culture devoted to delivering the best results to selected customers. Second, you'll note that the culture is reinforced by the right systems—measurement/control systems that keep things on track; reward systems that motivate people to live up to the commitment to their customers and encourage them in their quest for better results; and information systems that empower people to excel in those endeavors. Third, you will observe that they design their culture and systems around the right economic model. Those companies realize that a traditional economic model built on economies of scale and one-company accounting can't capture the nature of their successes or failures. Customer-intimate suppliers realize that standard pricing practices no longer make sense, because those procedures do not allow them to share in the profitable results they create for their customers. Fourth, profitable customer-intimate practices depend on the right start: That is, they find strong platforms to proceed from, and they move their organizations on toward greatness.

Now it's time to get down to specifics.

10 | SHAPE YOUR CULTURE

Behind every customer-intimate relationship, at least on the supplier's side, there is a strongly supportive corporate culture. In fact, I've found that the culture of a customer-intimate company—with its distinctive behaviors, beliefs, and mind-sets—is the single most important underpinning of successfully adopting the customer-intimate discipline. I have seen successful customer-intimate companies with less than stellar business processes, out-of-date technologies, inappropriate metrics, and shaky economic models, but never have I seen a customer-intimate company with a shallow or forgettable culture. Indeed, a strong culture can compensate for practically any weaknesses and deficiencies.

How do I know a strong culture when I see one? The signs are clear. First, the company has a memorable credo—a belief that permeates the company. Second, the credo is alive in three dominant themes of everyone's work life: judgment, cooperation, and learning.

Let's look at how this plays out.

FROM CREDO TO CULTURE

I had dinner some time ago with the former president of one of IBM's country operations. Talk turned to the question of the hour: What had gone wrong at Big Blue? The answer, according to my dinner companion, was quite simple: IBM had lost its soul. For decades the company had taken its bearings from the three-point credo established by its long-time boss Thomas Watson: respect the individual, look after the customer's well-being, and go the extra distance to assure the best results. But the company's commitment to those principles had weakened. The result was the decline of the most famous and successful customer-intimate corporation in history.

To an outsider, Watson's credo might sound like commercial piety. But to those inside IBM, it encapsulated what the company—and they, as employees of the company—stood for. That is no trivial matter, as Chairman John Foster of NovaCare points out. "I ask myself," he says, "why it is that so many of the companies I've worked for don't exist anymore, when other organizations like the Girl Scouts or the Bolshoi Ballet or the Marine Corps go on and on? My answer is that the other organizations stand for something."

Northwestern Mutual Life's statement of what it stands for goes back farther than IBM's—100 years—and is a good deal more succinct: "We exist for the benefit of our policyholders." President and CEO Jim Ericson declares: "What it says is that we are the policyholders' company. That's what mutual means—that we are owned by our customers. Everything we do—every decision we make—is based on what we think is good for our customers and our owners. It gives us a unique culture."

For specificity, however, few company credos are more direct than AutoZone's:

➤ AutoZoners always put customers first.

➤ We know our parts and products.

➤ Our stores look great.

➤ And we've got the best merchandise at the right price.

The only fuzziness here is the right price. It begs the question: Right for whom? Other that that, it's hard to imagine any Auto-Zone employee arguing with her boss, her colleague, or—for that matter—with a customer, over what exactly she should be doing or how she should be doing it. The above four slogans satisfy almost every requirement of a successful credo: They are doable, memorable, and unequivocal.

The process of bringing a credo to life usually starts with top management. I think of AutoZone's Buck Brown, vice president of human resources, customer satisfaction, for example, who tries to interact with customers as often as he can. He receives their complaints, takes the blame, and finds solutions. And more than once, I've heard customer-intimate executives cite the old adage that you can't move a piece of string by pushing the tail end of it. You have to get out front and pull.

But propagating the credo throughout the company isn't just the task of the senior executive. It's a responsibility that leaders at every level must take on. The three themes of workaday customer-intimate practice I mentioned above—judgment, cooperation, and learning—must virtually saturate the thoughts and actions of the entire enterprise. Judgment calls for everyone to be sensitive to the opportunities that are open to companies that are willing to serve many and varied customer needs. Cooperation isn't simply an imperative for building close customer connections, it's equally critical for establishing good working relations between front line and back office. Learning means recognizing that every interaction is the sustenance of a customer-intimate business, the fuel that keeps it moving—forward—to success.

USE YOUR JUDGMENT

Despite what I'll be saying in a minute about the necessity of front-line/back-office cooperation, the fact remains that in customer-intimate companies, employees who are in hands-on—or hand-to-hand—contact with their customers are effectively out there on their own. Every customer presents them with a different set of problems, and, except for the corporate mandate to deliver best solutions, they have no employee manual or standard operating procedures to fall back on. That means that they must use their own judgment in two senses, reactive and proactive. In the reactive sense, they have no choice: Their working conditions, their obligations to the company, and their own desire for success demand that they respond to changing market circumstances, to new needs and wants from the customer, and to new pressures from the back office, with independent, resourceful judgment. What else can they do, if they are to stay customer intimate?

But "use your judgment" has another, proactive sense. It means that frontline employees must have a keen eye for the commercial opportunities incipient in the variety and nuances of their customers' needs. It can be as simple as an AutoZone manager who recognizes that he should help his customer check for engine problems, or as complicated as a Degrémont manager who launches a study of local infrastructure, politics, and economics that may lead—years later—to a new water-purification plant. At the same time, however, the most successful customer-intimate companies make sure their people know how to deal with those opportunities. They don't get carried away. Some customers are simply wrong for the supplier. Some solutions don't play to the supplier's strengths. Thus judgment here demands discrimination, the ability to sort through opportunities to find those that are truly promising. And it demands an organization that supports such discrimination.

Mark E. Hamister, president and CEO of National Health Care Affiliates, describes his job as shaping a culture "for people to creatively exercise their entrepreneurial capabilities." And for his people to succeed, he adds, "They can't be stymied by a bureaucracy, approval process, or somebody's attitude that just because they have a bigger title, that makes them smarter." Clearly, as Hamister understands, a culture in which good commercial judgment flourishes is a culture of empowerment.

WORK TOGETHER

We've already discussed the importance of working with the customer. What we're addressing here is working together within your company, to prevent a disruption of the relationships between the company and its customers or among company insiders. In such industries as health care, for example, the customers' need for personal attention is vital. If you expect them to play games of bureaucratic hide-and-seek, you'll surely destroy intimacy. CIGNA HealthCare uses what regional director Maria Martinez calls a buddy system, which arranges for everyone who has person-to-person contact with customers to have a double who covers for him or her. "The person who sits next to me," she says, "is as familiar with my book of business as I am with hers. When I go on vacation, my buddy is just as capable of responding to issues on my desk as I will be when she goes on vacation."

The rifts between front and back offices, between sales and operations, are much more serious problems. Such rifts occur whenever sales, business development, or customer-service people, in their eagerness to please customers, make what the back-office personnel consider impossible, unprofitable, or just plain stupid commitments that they, in the back office, have to keep. Such situations can quickly deteriorate, with the back office viewing the frontline people as irresponsible idiots, and the frontline people viewing the back-office people as sluggards, or even outright saboteurs.

This situation is particularly apt to arise when a company is first beginning to move in a customer-intimate direction. Frontline employees may feel suddenly liberated, with a carte blanche to use their judgment to tailor solutions, coach customers, or partner with them. Meanwhile, back at the ranch, everyone is going crazy.

Part of the solution, and a spur to intimacy in itself, is to involve the back office, early on, in the search for results. Back-office staff, however, may well resist, as Bruce Grout of Airborne Express relates. "It took constant reinforcement at first," he says. "Unlike the past, they've had to get out, get in front of customers, and take part in the selling process."

Increasingly, successful customer-intimate companies prevent rifts by forming customer-service teams composed not just of sales and services people but of engineers, operations, and information-systems people as well. NCR Corporation uses dedicated multidisciplinary "Customer-Focused Teams" that design "Customer-Focused Solutions." Their terminology may feel ponderous, but the idea is right.

A company that works this way—with a culture of solidarity that binds all functions together—solves the problems of disconnection. Creating such a culture, in turn, means flattening the corporate hierarchy. Giving people authority to use their own judgment calls for transferring responsibility to them. Getting all team members to work toward well-understood and common goals makes supervisors superfluous and reduces dependence on central authority.

Flat hierarchies rely on modern information and communications technologies. The inverse is also true: Highly hierarchical companies stymie communications and information sharing. Striving for operational flexibility, Samsung Electronics slashed layers from its chain of command. Now, for example, the manager of the loading dock can easily speak directly with anyone else in the organization. Manager Richard Choi explains: "If anybody has any suggestions, he or she phones the VP or even the president. If the idea is good, they set up a meeting and we just do it."

Bollinger Industries is often even less formal. Pat Carrithers, vice president of marketing at Bollinger, says that his company is "incredibly flexible. We are a very unstructured company. Meetings tend to be what happens when you pass each other in the hallway. If customers have problems or questions, they don't have to work their way through a structure. They can go to the top. We have a small corps of top management people, and everybody shares the same vision and knowledge. If we add a lot of layers of management, task forces, and committees for this and middle managers of that, they would get busy slowing the process down."

WHAT CAN WE LEARN FROM THAT?

In the culture of customer intimacy, learning is a primary consideration: learning about customers and their needs, about potential solutions, and about structuring operations to improve results.

Airborne Freight Corporation holds seminars at its Seattle headquarters for its customer Nike. Nike's people spend two days getting

Airborne's "quick dose of the latest and greatest...in the air freight world." Though the evenings can be spent in so-called bonding activities, the days are dedicated to educating the customer at the supplier's initiative and expense. And everyone benefits.

At Nypro, the plastics-injection company, customer demands come fast and furious. Customers look for "much, much stronger capability: on-site tooling, one-stop shopping, and faster product development," says Daniel Meek, vice president. Nypro aims for a "multifaceted" relationship with the customer. The regional sales-people deal with their local procurement people; our market development people deal with their market development people; and so on, and so on, all the way to the top, to senior management," says Randall S. Barko, corporate vice president, marketing and sales.

LEVERAGE HUMAN RESOURCES

A strong combination of good recruitment, hiring procedures, and training curricula gives customer-intimate business leaders real leverage on their culture.

From the point of view of a job hunter, interviewing for a role in a customer-intimate enterprise is a distinctive experience. Of course the recruit will respond to the usual inquiries about skills, employment background, business smarts, and so on. But on top of that, the nature of the discipline being what it is, the customer-intimate company will focus on more ambiguous qualities. Degrémont, the water-treatment company, puts a premium on finding people with a sense of adventure and global curiosity. That represents a break from the conventional practice of French firms to view graduation from a prestigious school as a strong qualification. What Robbie Bach, Microsoft's director of marketing, desktop applications division, wants to know is whether an applicant "...is creative about issues and problems and has good communication skills." He asks many prospects to describe the most challenging interpersonal problem they have ever faced. Bach is less interested in applicants' answers than in how nimbly they handle the questions. "I give people points for counterintuitive answers," he says.

Customer-intimate training programs have a unique flavor. They commonly emphasize problem-solving, teamwork, and innovation instead of the individual mastery of codified skills. At customer-intimate companies, employees train one another. They rarely defer to training departments.

At Nypro, boards of directors, comprising managers from Nypro's entire organization, assist people in its plants throughout the world. Everyone shares the insight that comes from different geographic points of view. Nypro's sales and marketing people have training and experience in operations or engineering. "When they deal with customers," says vice president Randall S. Barko, "They bring value right there."

Northwestern Mutual Life has a comparable approach to training. In an industry notorious for its turnover of salespeople, Northwestern Mutual stands above the crowd. By the time they have two to four years of experience with Northwestern, the agents attend a two-week career school where, in the words of Robert E. Carlson, executive vice president, marketing, they "put the edge...on their sales techniques and technical knowledge of the business." But while they're sharpening their skills, many of those agents will form study groups to exchange ideas about "selling, how products work, how they find people, how they keep records, how they manage their finances, and how they manage the strain, if you will, of raising a family and building a business at the same time." Northwestern provides other such learning situations throughout the agents' careers, up to and including preparation for retirement. "We're in this business for the long term," says Carlson. "We bring our agents into the business to be in it for the long term, and we try to treat them as entrepreneurs and independent businesspeople."

Such cross-training leads to the cross-fertilization of ideas, enhancing knowledge, engendering cooperation, and encouraging the judgments that make customer-intimate organizations such lively settings for commercial imagination and the pursuit of best-delivered results.

HOW ARE WE DOING?

No company creates its culture overnight: It takes persistence and time to turn a credo of intimacy into the values, beliefs, and actions that bind an organization together. To what dangers should managers be alert as they move forward? How can they gauge their progress?

Several signs clearly show a culture that falls short of intimacy. The most obvious is employees' balky attitude or lack of enthusiasm for establishing close relations with customers or taking responsibility for results. Such employees measure customer relations in terms of 10-foot poles. "We do our thing," they believe. "They do theirs." "We take our cues from customers: If they don't ask for total solutions, I don't see how we can force them to accept ours."

Companies with negative attitudes toward internal cooperation will also show slow progress. Check whether everyone in the organization focuses on common objectives. How well is the sales organization aligned with the goals of manufacturing and operations? Do prospects extol the proposals of your salespeople when, unfortunately, manufacturing has never been organized to deliver on their promises? Is the frontline service trained and equipped to live up to the promises of advertising campaigns? Do distributors and dealers agree with the supplier's people about everyone's responsibilities in their cooperative creation of the best value for customers?

Managerial resistance to adopting a truly flexible stance toward customers' needs and desires is another problem. Meeting customers' needs with customized solutions is an essential aspect of a customer-intimate policy, and certain managers find it untenable. Those people prefer to deal with an orderly and predictable world, where one's duty is reduced to repeating identical tasks. Variety and diversity, and the attendant uncertainty, are upsetting. Most people don't want to admit that they dislike uncertainty, and they rationalize their opposition with such arguments as "Variety kills efficiency; we'd lose our economies of scale." They resist tailoring because "It sounds like a recipe for losing money on every single transaction." Or they believe that "Customers are fickle: By the time we figure out what to customize and how to personalize, they'll have changed their mind." For these managers, the practice of business agility is the equivalent of a life sentence to Outward Bound. Meanwhile, of course, the best-cultivated companies bound ahead of them. They conquer the challenges rather than bemoan them.

11 | MOLD YOUR SYSTEMS

New technologies aren't simply new answers to old questions, they also present new questions we never thought to ask and answers we never thought we needed. Business technology is a terrific example of that phenomenon. Businesses can deploy information systems that gather, remember, retrieve, manipulate, and circulate just about all collections of data anywhere. And they do.

One result of those enormously expanded capabilities has been a mania for metrics. So I do feel a certain reluctance to propose—as I'm about to do—a whole new metrical agenda. But the fact is that the discipline of customer intimacy demands measurement systems distinct from those of the disciplines of operational excellence or product leadership.

At operationally excellent companies, the metrics are primarily process-oriented. They measure the time and other costs of accomplishing certain tasks, with a view to containment. Those businesses track defects—indicators of inefficiencies and waste—to get a fix on customer satisfaction in terms of preestablished standards. Product-leadership companies emphasize metrics that are in line with their goals. They want to know the dimensions of their current pool of new ideas and technologies, how much time it takes to develop an idea into a commercially viable product, how much the specs of particular products have improved, how much time it takes to establish a new product in the market, the level of acceptance among targeted customers, the product's profitability, and so on.

MEASURE THE RIGHT THINGS

All this makes sense if you want to track return on investment and customer satisfaction as traditionally defined. The trouble is, customer-intimate enterprises can't afford the limitations of traditional definitions. That's because companies, by dedicating themselves to providing better and better results for their customers, also commit themselves to a new kind of double-entry bookkeeping. They've got to track not only their own results but their customers' as well. A customer-intimate company, in other words, can't discover how it's doing merely by drawing up an account of its own assets, liabilities, and possibilities. It must also look to the assets and liabilities of the businesses with which it has chosen to link its time, efforts, money, imagination—and fate.

Easy enough, you say, if the supplier has direct access to its customers' books. But what if it doesn't, or, as is more likely in all but the most intimate relationships, has only limited access? Enter the imperatives of the new metrical agenda, with its indirect measures and its measures of the relationship.

Track Retention

This measure is as crucial as the subscription-renewal rate in the magazine publishing business, says Gabe Battista, the CEO of Cable & Wireless, Inc.: "We measure by retention of customers. Ultimately, you win or lose based on what percentage of your customers you keep. In a service business...a 1 percent difference in retention—positive or negative—has a phenomenal leverage impact on your bottom line. We have been able to keep our retention at a 98 percent level, above our industry average."

Monitor Share-of-Customer

In addition, rather than measuring the customer's own market share (the total amount of business it has in a specific industry or market segment divided by the total amount of business all suppliers have in that customer's market) customer-intimate companies track the amount of business they get from a specific client and divide that into the total business this client is giving to all its suppliers. A customer-intimate company might also compare the growth of its business with a particular client with the overall growth of the client's business with all its suppliers. A growth rate of 10 percent, with a customer whose total business purchases have increased only 5 percent, indicates a higher level of penetration into that customer's affairs. Clearly, Airborne's growing involvement in Nike's business—after the difficulties we saw in an earlier chapter—provides a sound measure of success.

Find Other Evidence of Results

Measurement is the basis of promise-making. Jeananne Digan, manager of new business integration for CIGNA Retirement & Investment Services, speaks confidently of the range of offerings her company proposes to prospective clients. "What we want to be able to do is to go to a prospect and say, 'Given this plan design and our communications programs, you will generate X percent increase in employee participation in the retirement plan.'"

Her confidence derives from a rich and varied system of tracking and analysis that includes case studies, gathering information in enrollment seminars, and monitoring the effect of asset allocation. Those are the hard, quantitative measures. There are measures, too, that include focus groups, direct feedback from salespeople who meet with clients, and the client research the company performs every 18 months or so.

Staples and one of its largest customers, Ameritech, cooperate on feedback and assessment. In fact, it's Ameritech, the customer, that tracks Staples' accuracy in filling its orders—the "good, bad, and ugly"—as Debbie Wozniak, Ameritech's director of procurement, puts it. Traditionally, that role would have been played by Staples itself, but since Ameritech is the ultimate user, it naturally has the evidence to activate improvement plans.

This is not to say that Staples doesn't track its own measurements. For example, First Fidelity Bank, another Staples customer, notes that service time for office supplies improved dramatically, from two weeks to 24 hours. Eulanda Brooks, a vice president at First Fidelity, says, "I measure the number of complaints to determine what kind of service level we're getting." Complaints are few—no more than one or two per month.

And sometimes indices of failing intimacy with a customer are so obvious, they practically wag a finger in your face. Lori Lucy, materials manager, Diagnostic Instrument Corp., says she does nothing fancy to track success. "I can tell by how well I am able to service my customers. If the machines are always down, and we are always running out of parts, it's not going so well."

Put Customer Performance in Perspective

Customer-intimate companies try to get straight to the point—the other guy's point. Precisely how much did the customer's performance improve as a result of their association? How does that gain compare with its competitors' benchmarks? In many industrial businesses, you can monitor the clients' performances by examining their process performance, cost performance, etc. Nypro, for instance, can more readily quantify the effect it has had on Vistakon's or on Abbott's operations. It assesses those accounts in terms of their product development time: the time it takes to ramp up a production line to deal with, say, unanticipated, rapidly increasing demand.

For a customer-intimate company to determine its specific impact on a customer, and share that information with the customer, is valuable in more ways than one. Within the company, it keeps everyone focused on what is most important—results—while providing the customer with hard, tangible measurements of benefit. In fact, all regular monitoring of the client's business creates a scorecard of results that enhances the meaningfulness of the connection and spurs both parties to higher levels of performance.

For example, because of their intimate connection, Diagnostic Instrument and Marshall Industries collaborate on their forecasting and share information on overhead and cost drivers. Marshall's line of credit allowed Diagnostic to expand, creating greater opportunity for both companies. Such results flow from trust. James F. Hashem, president of Diagnostic, says, "We no longer give Marshall's people purchase orders. We give them a forecast. They trust the relationship enough that they put the material into the store against the forecast, and we draw it out. We have eliminated purchase orders and invoices. The computerized listing of what we've taken out of the store becomes our invoice."

Track Your Own Profitability

Finally, in case you were wondering whether customer intimacy requires companies to fixate on their customers' minutiae to the exclusion of their own details, let me emphasize that this is not the case. The last critical measure is one that monitors the supplier's results.

In effect, customer-intimate businesses account for the so-called lifetime value of a customer. That means estimating the costs and revenues of a given relationship over the time you expect that customer to be yours. Costs, not incidentally, include time, effort, and imagination that go into getting to know the customer and customizing the ways in which you will address their business.

When you've judged the risk involved in pursuing a customer's business, you can decide whether that customer is right for you. Thereafter, you can continuously monitor the client's revenues, costs, and the expected length of the relationship to determine if your initial judgment was accurate and to improve the picture.

But regardless of the sophistication of your measurements and interpretations, up-to-date, continually refined knowledge of the revenue stream and associated costs can prevent the unpleasant surprises that sour a business connection.

LEVERAGE YOUR INFORMATION SYSTEMS

These days even the corner convenience store has a computer system that functions both as a cash register and an inventory-control system. The integration of technology with business is permanent and ubiquitous. In a customer-intimate company, information technology provides unique dimensions of value. But it must be right in both design and application. What many companies discover as they begin moving in a customer-intimate direction is that their technology—superb in its own terms—is unwieldy when it comes to the fine art of customer intimacy.

Traditionally, the goal of information technology systems was to help companies maintain standardized operations and economies of scale. Low cost and reliability were key requirements, not speed or flexibility. Fragmentation and functional optimization, rather than integration, were the norm. The aim of systems design was to control internal operations: Customer information was limited to order management and financial record-keeping. Technology that captured the richness of specific customers' profiles or that facilitated close customer connections was not a consideration. As a result, large-scale, inflexible systems and technology are still common. Although they serve their original functions, they prove a hindrance in a customer-intimate connection.

The customer-intimate company is a new kind of organism. It thrives on fine-grain distinctions and broad diversity rather than standardization. It cooperates rather than competes. It thrives on knowledge expansion and growth, not on routinization. So it must design an informational nervous system that can register the fluctuations and effects of that spirit. In customer-intimate companies, technology enables and empowers in three distinct ways: by facilitating precision management, by linking everyone and everything together, and by slaking the thirst for knowledge and learning.

Manage with Precision

Information systems and technology greatly assist the customer-intimate organization by providing highly detailed information on each individual customer situation—including the measures and metrics described above. In-depth information about customers and about experiences with those customers in a range of situations was simply not available even a few years ago.

Think, for example, of Uni Storebrand, the leading Norwegian insurance company, which now keeps between 100 and 200 pieces of information on each of its more than one million customers. Or consider the huge volume of detailed information a company like water purifier Degrémont captures. Degrémont spends years monitoring marketplaces in which a potential customer might emerge. Northwestern Mutual Life's Personal Planning Analysis covers the gamut of a customer's needs—life insurance, college planning for children, annuities, disability, retirement—and yields more detailed information about the customer than perhaps even his or her best friend knows.

Northwestern has a similarly intimate view of the nature of its customer relationships: who's buying what, what their ages are, what buyers' incomes are, whether they are repeat buyers, etc. "The company," says Dick Hall, senior vice president for corporate planning, "talks to policyholders right after they buy, policy owners who have been with us a while, policyholders who are leaving us, and even people who have been approached by our agents who have chosen not to be policyholders." Hall believes that it is "not enough to know whether your customers are satisfied. You need to know what they are satisfied with and what is important to them."

You can enrich grainy information of this sort by sharing it throughout your organization so that every department can make contributions, comments, or corrections on the information contained in specific client records.

But those high-detail records are not limited to customer information. They also contain situational information: a record of actual situations in the past and a projection of possible situations in the future. Moreover, they include idiosyncratic interpretations, nuanced commentaries, and reasoned speculation from everyone involved. And, of course, in a customer-intimate company such true-to-human-life information also serves an important function in calibrating the measurements described earlier in this chapter.

Customer-intimate companies need moment-to-moment readings of the customer pulse. They must be able to gauge, at any time, how effectively specific processes are delivering value. Just as important, everyone with a need to know must have access to all this information and knowledge—to provide greater responsiveness, to tailor the production or servicing process, to enhance marketing or business development, or to improve interaction with customers.

Use Technology as a Cohesive Force

Information systems permit the coordination of the various parts of an organization so that, for example, rifts are avoided between the front and back office. Those systems provide the principal link between suppliers and customers who need to share information and evaluation. Those two essential functions can, of course, assume a great variety of guises. We have seen how Nypro's information systems linked its manufacturing processes with the offices of such customers as Vistakon. AutoZone's computers maintain inventory status and customer information at all of its retail outlets. When repeat customers call a store, any store, their records are instantly available.

Technology helps bind customer relationships. Don Smith, vice president and general manager of Sky Courier, an Airborne subsidiary, illustrates the point perfectly. System-1, his company's on-line reservation system, was the first in the air freight business. "Because time is so important to our customers," he says, "we had to have a way to quote flights. Once the customer has presented us with the problem—the origin and destination cities—we had to find a way to quote a flight within seconds." System-1 provided the way. Without that technology, the company would have been unable to fulfill front-office promises; if it hadn't kept promises, it wouldn't have established trust; and without trust, it would never have established intimacy.

Another illustration: James F. Hashem, president of Diagnostic Instrument, tells us that customers phone to amend their orders. They might say, "I know you promised us 100 printed circuit boards next week, but I could use 125." In the past, he says, "that question used to take us weeks to answer because we would have to go out and see if we could get an extra 25 sets of parts. We would have to visit a bill of materials line by line and check every single part. Because we're keeping Marshall inventory in our Marshall store, we can punch a few keys, and within an hour, our shared computer system gives us an answer to the customers' questions."

Information systems can serve as a consensus builder to create alignment. Everybody has access to the same information; therefore, nobody wastes time reconciling information. Everybody sings from the same hymnal.

Open Up the Font of Learning

Within a customer-intimate company, information technology and systems empower the organization through the learning process. This is hardly front-page news, but in a customer-intimate enterprise, a learning organization par excellence, it's not trivial news, either. The promise, the value proposition, of customer intimacy is the delivery of best results. The better job the company has done learning about the customer—its needs and desires, its commercial world—the better its solutions and its results.

Technology certainly enables sounder forecasting. What's true for circuit boards holds for motor oil as well. Information technology utterly transformed AutoZone's inventory control and forecasting ability. Its old system used an information system that Clete Faddis, district manager, Macon, Georgia district, says, was "just a memory box. You'd go up to each shelf and key in the part number that identified the product. It took me about 20 hours a week to order for my store. At that time, there were about 300 stores in the chain, so we had 300 managers spending 20 hours a week ordering for their stores. Plus you had 300 different opinions on the right way to order for your store." Sometimes people guessed right, he says, but more often stores ended up with excess inventory tying up money or lost sales through stock outages. When the company switched to its new computer system, the changes were enormous and immediate. An eight-week forecasting cycle was built into the software. It was subtle enough to factor in the weather, for example, which has a direct impact on antifreeze sales. Order time dropped dramatically, first to less than two hours and, in some cases, to less than 25 minutes. "You know where those extra 20 hours of mine went?" asks Faddis. "I was in front of my customers."

Scania, the Swedish heavy truck and vehicle manufacturer, and Black & Decker, the toolmaker, use information technology to play "what if" games: "If a specific part fails prematurely, what options would we have in switching our manufacturing processes or task-sequencing to free up capacity to deal with that eventuality?" Cable & Wireless, Inc. has a "user-friendly database" called "SNAP," which keeps files up to date by instantly logging the last "comment, question, or concern that the customer had," says CEO Gabe Battista. This allows a rep to say, "I see that you called up with a question about our new international service to such and such a country.

While I have you on the line, did that work the way that it was supposed to? Are you using it? Are you fully aware of how it works? Technology allows true seamless service," says Battista.

It allows, in fact, customer intimacy. Period. If good information is the foundation of responsible promise-making, and if responsible promise-making is the foundation of trust, and if trust is the foundation of customer-supplier intimacy, then technology is the fundamental basis of the practice of customer intimacy. Without it, customer intimacy could never be more than the local shopkeeper variety, where you're known by name and people remember your tastes. Without systems for dealing with the mounting complexity generated by increasing numbers of specific customers and specific requirements—not to mention the constantly changing market conditions—customer intimacy cannot rise above the cottage industry level. Customer intimacy, the ultimate niche strategy, is simply unthinkable without sophisticated technological capabilities: not only sophisticated, but right for the task and the customer.

AGAIN, HOW ARE WE DOING?

There are three sets of questions I ask companies aspiring to customer intimacy. The first is about customer results: Do you truly know how you've affected the customer's results? If you do, do you measure this on a regular basis, in tangible terms, and do you share that set of measurements with the customer? And, perhaps trickiest and most important of all, does the customer agree with the interpretation?

It's easy to imagine a case in which the customer doesn't buy the supplier's assessment of impact. The natural tendency is always to overstate one's contribution. Customer-intimate companies avoid such troublesome ambiguities and disagreements by generating data that so crisply and accurately reflects the reality that the customer cannot help but accept the assessment. And the nice added benefit is that the same data for measuring outcomes and results can be tied to the rewards for teams and individuals within the customer-intimate company itself.

The second set of questions relates, precisely, to reward and incentive systems: Have the ways you measure and motivate people been properly designed to deliver superior results and retain customers? Do they encourage teamwork both internally and with intermediaries and customers? Do they track customers' business over more than a single transaction? Do they attract and retain the right kinds of employees? The key rewards—bonuses, raises, promotions—flowing from those measurements must reflect the attainment of better results for customers.

The last set of questions pertains to the company's use of technology: Is it set up to reinforce the culture of judgment, cooperation, and learning? Does it provide the level of substance, timeliness, and ease-of-use that allows the company's measurement, control, and reward systems to deliver results?

Ask yourself these questions—continuously, courageously, and comprehensively—and you will always know where you've been, where you are, and how far you've still got to go in the practice of customer intimacy.

12 | ADAPT YOUR ECONOMICS

Frequently people ask me, "How can customer-intimate companies offer truly exceptional, individually designed solutions to so many different customers without going broke?" They ask that question because they assume that to make money they need to build economies of scale and streamlined transactions. Such conventional thinking makes perfect sense for those pursuing mass markets with standardized products. But customer-intimate tailoring undermines economies of scale, and elaborate, premium services are anything but low-cost.

Conventional thinking overlooks two essential aspects of customer intimacy. First, what counts is the payoff of the long-term relationship—not the profit from individual transactions. Second, the point of customer intimacy is that suppliers and customers win together. The whole approach relies on their cooperating to enlarge the economic pie that they ultimately share. Thus, to see how a customer-intimate company makes money, we have to shift our thinking from traditional economics of transactions to an entirely different model—the economics of cooperation.

To get the new economics right, the parties must—first and foremost—find ways through tailoring, coaching, and/or partnering to make the supplier-customer connection productive. As we've seen in earlier chapters, cooperative behavior at this level can generate a variety of new financial benefits for both customer and supplier. Next, the supplier must get a handle on the costs of delivering results for its customers. Companies steeped in the traditional model of transaction economics will find it difficult to analyze the intricacies of cooperation and accurately evaluate the costs. Finally, after they take into account the benefits and price tag of cooperation, customer and supplier must determine how to divvy up their net gains—through pricing, or other creative and innovative means.

Let's take a closer look at each determinant of our new economic model.

SEARCH FOR THE BENEFITS OF COOPERATION

Remember how Procter & Gamble and Wal-Mart put aside their mutual apprehensions and forged a connection that cut redundancies in inventory, logistics, and order management processes? The benefits of their boldness were evident: Their cooperation reduced the sizable costs of their earlier win–lose interactions. In general, people who don't know one another well operate on a certain level of caution or even distrust. Each scrutinizes the other, building caution and safeguards into the relationship. While such wariness is understand-able and sometimes even prudent, it can blind both parties to the potentially enormous benefits of cooperative behavior.

What are those benefits? Consider the huge effort buyers and sellers expend in freewheeling, competitive marketplaces where every transaction is hard-won, and loyalty is nonexistent. In such environments customers turn to many suppliers, pitting one against another, ostensibly to keep everyone honest. No matter that there's little incentive for suppliers to pull out all the stops for their cus-tomers. No matter that evidence demonstrates the huge advantages of supplier rationalization, an alternative approach in which cus-tomers opt to work more closely with fewer, selected vendors.

Xerox, as I mentioned in Chapter 8, for example, is much better off since it reduced its supplier base in the 1980s. The automotive industry has also consolidated its supplier base. Over the past decade, Ford cut more than half of its suppliers and plans to further reduce today's 2,300 suppliers even more by the year 2000. Peugeot-Citroën, the French carmaker, has already cut 1,400 suppliers from its long list of 2,200, and by the end of this century, it will reduce the total to 500 suppliers.

Those companies have found that more extensive connections with fewer suppliers eliminates unpredictable fluctuations in price, creates more stability by enhancing ongoing relationships, fosters an atmosphere of cooperative problem-solving, and ultimately boosts profits across the board.

Consider the folly of having a supplier perform an outgoing inspection only to have the customer repeat that effort with an incoming check. With trust and cooperation, the two companies can cut the inspection work—and its expense—in half. Consider cus-tomers that stockpile inventory for fear that their suppliers won't fill orders in time. The suppliers, in turn, build buffer stocks to make sure they don't get caught empty-handed by unpredictable customers.

With closer cooperation, both can reduce the costs of maintaining excess, just-in-case, insurance-policy-style inventory.

James F. Hashem, president of Diagnostic Instrument Corporation enthusiastically extols the virtues of his company's relationship with Marshall Industries. "The trust factor is unbelievable. Customer and vendor sit down together to ensure the vendor is making money, a pretty rare and wonderful arrangement. They go into detail: 'What costs you money? What can we do to lower the overhead?'"

Hashem describes how Diagnostic rationalized Marshall's billing system. "Their standard way of operating was to cut an invoice every time a transaction came from their stockroom. They stuck the invoice in an envelope, stamped it, and mailed it to us. My people in accounting were slitting 300 envelopes a week, entering 300 pieces of data into our computer, and tracking all that accounts billable information. My materials manager said, 'This is crazy. Why don't we set up a weekly billing? We'll consolidate all the transactions, summarize them on a computer report, and generate one cover invoice.' Now there's one envelope we have to open, one piece of data we enter into the computer, and one piece of data we have to track. I've gone from $6 million in sales to $33 million in sales and I still have only two people in accounting. That's where you start to make money. It's not coming out of my profit margin or out of Marshall's: It's coming out of our costs. The partnership has been tremendous for our customers because we've been able to lower our cost and offer better service."

Cooperation also allows for improvements in work allocations. Shifting certain tasks from customer to supplier, as several of our tailoring examples illustrated, or from supplier to customer, as we saw in coaching, benefits both. In some situations, the pragmatic solution calls for sharing responsibility for tasks. Certain transactions don't need to meet rigid deadlines. Because of their cooperative relationship, the supplier and the customer are well-positioned to establish which work can be spread over time, postponed to a later date, and handled when most appropriate.

Just as they benefit from parceling out work to the most suitable party, cooperating suppliers and customers can also collaborate on investment decisions. Sometimes it's best for the supplier to make an investment that benefits both partners. On occasion the customer, alone or with the supplier, should undertake the business risk. Bruce Grout of Airborne reflects. "Years ago, without a very specific, concrete contract, you'd never make a joint investment. Today, with certain kinds of business, we're willing to say, 'Hey, this is where the future should be going. Let's try to partner with this customer. We'll make the investment and see where it takes us.' The customer must be what I would call a young, aggressive, growing company, willing to take similar risks in the project. They have to agree to put in the necessary systems and management time in order to bring it all together. When we find a company like that, the whole endeavor operates smoothly. Everyone is working together and looking for mutual rewards."

Finally, there is one other important benefit of working cooperatively: Such cooperative undertakings encourage learning on both sides. When supplier and customer understand one another's concerns, each can clearly attune itself to the other's requirements. The supplier, with its deep knowledge of the customer's situation, profits financially because it can target its products and services: No more wasteful shotgun approaches. The well-connected supplier needs never overservice low-value customers and segments or, worse yet, spend time and resources to service customers who are not right for its business.

Overall, knowledge of each individual customer generates clear economic benefits that suppliers can use to forecast and streamline operations. As we've seen, AutoZone doesn't stock parts for every car model. It keys its inventory to the age, make, and models that predominate in the trading area of each store.

UNDERSTAND YOUR COST DYNAMICS

As I've said, the economics of cooperation differ from the traditional model of transaction economics. This is particularly evident in the way customer-intimate companies view their costs. Because their products and services are individually designed, it makes no sense to average costs. Instead, such companies gear their accounting toward calculating the costs of every offering, or, more specifically, the costs of serving a particular customer over an extended period of time.

All that's further complicated: Customer-intimate companies cannot treat overhead charges in traditional ways. Such charges— headquarters expenses, the expenses of the service department or other shared facilities and features—aren't directly attributable to an individual offering or customer. The traditional way to allocate overhead charges is to spread them evenly across the board: The traditional supplier adds equal charges to the cost of serving customer A and customer B, even if customer A's product requires far more extensive tailoring or embellishments. Customer A's product looks inexpensive to make, and before long, its price reflects that artificially low cost. In the same vein, the cost of customer B's simpler product will look artificially high, and it may end up with an inappropriately inflated price tag that B will certainly resent.

Misallocation of overhead charges distorts prices and, by extension, the value that each customer receives. I've seen this repeatedly in such businesses as chemical companies, where products range from the very basic to the specialties typically marketed in a customer-intimate mode. Biased accounting methods yield price distortions that disrupt the calculations of lifetime value and other economics associated with customer intimacy. Those distortions might lead a company to conclude incorrectly that some (truly valuable) customers or particular business initiatives aren't adequately profitable.

I know of companies that have successfully adopted such methods as activity-based costing to deal with that issue. In essence, they aim for a realistic estimate of each activity's true costs, rather than looking at expenses in the aggregate. Others set prices based on the product's value to the customer, instead of the supplier's cost. If Customer A negotiated a $100 price for its fancy product, and Customer B paid only $50 for its plain version, the supplier allocates overhead charges in a 2:1 proportion. Either approach has its merits.

The other complicating factor in the economics of cooperation—a positive one this time—is that cooperative connections actually reduce certain costs. Because the supplier doesn't sell and resell its customers, its business development and selling expenses go way down: Customers remain committed unless the supplier fails to deliver promised results. Likewise, suppliers don't pile on expenses when they expand business with a close, loyal customer. It takes some ingenuity to quantify such cost advantages, but several business researchers have shown us that it is doable. British Airways calculated that it costs 6 times less to keep a valued customer than to acquire a new customer. Their statistics aren't atypical even though specific numbers vary from situation to situation.

Don't discount the value of your loyal customers' free advertising. Their endorsements and laudatory referrals—especially their praise for the tangible results they've amassed from their relationship with you, the supplier—are more credible than any paid advertising. Though word of mouth is hard to quantify, it's enormously important, and that's why customer-intimate companies frequently use customers' testimonials to support their promotions.

Finally, another way customer-intimate suppliers save costs is in their customers' tolerance of mishaps and other delivery difficulties. Customers recognize that certain kinds of problems provide grist for the learning mill. The experiences teach the supplier how to deliver better performance. Customer and supplier work together to resolve difficulties, and together they reduce service-recovery costs.

DIVVY UP THE GAINS

In customer-intimate circles I often hear people say, "Let's be fair and equitable." They know that the name of the game is winning together rather than advancing at the expense of the other party. Finding a way to make both customer and supplier feel that their cooperation has been, and will continue to be, worthwhile is the final variable in the economic equation. Divvying up the gains comes down to pricing and terms.

Setting prices that reflect the added value to each customer is an excellent way to share the gains. Companies do this, for example, by charging a premium for the tailored solutions they provide, or by levying a fee for their coaching. They practice value-based, pay-for-performance pricing.

Often, companies fail to adopt such practices because they are trapped in the traditional economies-of-scale mind-set. They pursue scale economies to drive down costs, and then add a standard markup on top to determine their prices. They don't distinguish among customers when they price their products and services. Their cost-plus-markup prices fail to account for varying levels of results or varying levels of appreciation for those results. So customers end up believing that the prices are too high or, even, too low. Neither outcome contributes to a long-term win–win connection. That's why this approach is anathema to companies that practice true customer intimacy.

Another complication arises when a supplier prices individual parts of its product separately. While this might seem to offer flexibility and choice, in reality, it directs the customer's mind from buying a total solution—the essence of intimacy. Customers may well be tempted to compare prices and start shopping for better deals on individual components, and that undermines the customer-intimate connection.

Bundled pricing may be an appropriate way to keep the customer's mind on the broader solution. Package low-margin and high-margin components together at a fair price that reflects the value the customer gets. Likewise, the supplier may suggest a contract that covers multiple transactions over time and minimizes fluctuations in profit margin from one purchase to the next. It's like a restaurant that offers its regulars a fixed-fee menu, even though its margins fluctuate daily. When a customer-intimate company's new-account start-up costs are high, it could spread out those initial charges by building them into the contract price. Such practices surely simplify the pricing and purchasing process, saving time and effort for both seller and buyer.

My message here is that the supplier's offering must provide a total solution that creates results for the customer. The supplier should work backward asking, "What are all the components of the solution that I need to bundle into this offering?" If it takes additional inducement for the customer to buy into that total solution—say an attractive, all-in-one price for the full range of components of the solution—so be it.

Stay Clear of Cross-Subsidizing

The decision to go for bundled pricing rather than piecemeal pricing is, however, less than clear-cut. When a company's offerings are a mixture of standard and customer-specific products, the pricing dilemma grows more complex. Consider a bank that caters to a customer who, 90 percent of the time, wants a standard, best-total-cost offering. The customer wants flawless, quick service at the lowest possible cost. But 1 time in 10, the customer expects premium services: a nonroutine wire transfer, help in sorting out a messy checkbook, or advice with financial planning. It's tempting to placate such a customer by having standard services cross-subsidize the premium customer-intimate treatment. But that's a bad idea: The customer wins, but the bank loses. If, to help defray the costs of such intimate treatment, the bank raises its fees across the board, it effectively forces all customers—even the least demanding—to pay for special services.

The same thing happens in the industrial arena. A paper or chemical company with lines of standard and specialty offerings that require totally different pricing sometimes yields to customer pressures and treats everything as a single business. Either the supplier's profitability suffers, or the standardized-product buyers end up subsidizing the specialty-product buyers. Of course, in fiercely competitive markets, the latter is a short-term scenario: Buyers of the standardized product will quickly find a better deal elsewhere.

In that case, as in the case of the bank, there are ways to escape the economic quagmire. Begin by considering whether you can change your customer's expectations and, at the same time, your pricing policy. At the bank, that could mean requiring the demanding customer to pay for the premium services. Why not institute a premium-service fee? A number of well-known banks charge customers several dollars when they use in-person teller services rather than the automated teller machines. For the paper and chemical companies, it means charging buyers for what they buy, based on a true understanding of the economics of the standard and the specialty lines. No more cross-subsidizing: People get what they pay for.

Beyond that, the bank and the industrial company may well need to disentangle their disparate offerings and their associated economics. It might be best to treat each offering as a separate branch, creating a clear demarcation between what, in essence, are operationally excellent businesses and customer-intimate businesses. Only then can the supplier ask how best to deliver on the distinctive value proposition of each branch and what pricing policies would allow fair and equitable sharing of gains.

Make Your Economics Revealing

Once a company ascertains the true economics of all pricing situations, its business decisions may take a significant turn. Customers that previously appeared to be most attractive are no longer so appealing. Quite often, a supplier regards big customers as critical until it understands the economics. Similarly, small accounts, once perceived as easy to serve, may reveal themselves as drains on a company's time and resources. Thoroughly assessing the economics of various customers may alter your assumptions about which are attractive and which are not. Once you get down to brass tacks, you will need to revise the generalizations that, for many years, have guided your company.

Another assumption that may call for revision is that setting the right price is the best or only way to share the gains of cooperation. More and more, companies true to the spirit of customer intimacy are making gain-sharing arrangements of a more complicated nature. Their logic is straightforward: If the supplier commits itself to its customers' results, its rewards should be directly coupled with those results. The interdependency of supplier and customer extends itself to the supplier's compensation.

In its simple form, companies express that logic in their results-guaranteed pledge. Return the product if you don't like it, and we'll give you back your money. The customer-intimate company exceeds such promises by truly putting its fate in the hands of its customers.

Consider Young & Rubicam (Y&R), which, for a time, was Colgate-Palmolive's major—but not its sole—ad agency. In 1995, Colgate gave Y&R all of its advertising business. Y&R, in turn, expressed its commitment by tying a portion of its compensation to the effectiveness of its communications solutions. In advertising, such arrangements are increasingly replacing fixed-fee contracts and straight commissions on billings.

Gain-sharing contracts are on the rise in other industries as well. Baxter Healthcare has risk-sharing agreements with its hospital clients; Vought Aircraft Co. is experimenting with revenue-sharing arrangements; Honda and Nissan have worked out ways to inspire such suppliers as Donnelley Corp. (mirrors), Asea Brown Boveri (paint), and Clarion (radios) to deliver better results.

In the spirit of cooperation, many companies don't carve their pricing practices, contracts, and arrangements in stone. They modify them when changing circumstances make change advisable. But even if such flexibility softens potential exposure, there's no sense denying that a lot is at stake. The upshot of all this is that the fortunes of suppliers and customers are increasingly interconnected. And that's why understanding every facet of the economics of cooperation is a critical linchpin when companies compete intimately.

13 | WHERE DO YOU START?

When most of us sit down to make New Year's resolutions, we examine our flaws and vow to correct them as the starting point of a more productive and fruitful life. This might explain why many managers intuitively conclude that addressing weaknesses and perceived shortcomings is the best way to approach the challenges and opportunities of intimacy. "If we fix this," they decide, "we'll be halfway there."

After investigating dozens of successful customer-intimate companies, I'm convinced that examining strengths, not weaknesses, is the most effective way to start the journey. The foundation of intimacy is already there—in what you do exceptionally well. You then build upon it by transforming highly developed skills into customer-intimacy skills. Although no two companies approach intimacy from exactly the same angle, four areas of business expertise make for effective starting points for the journey: competence in operations, product development skills, strong customer affinity or consulting expertise, and prowess in general contracting or brokering.

Competence in Operations

In business environments with stringent standards for operations, shrewd companies leverage the systems they already have in place to broaden the solutions for individual customers. CIGNA HealthCare and Staples, for example, found that trying to gain competitive advantage solely by focusing on costs severely restricted their growth opportunities. If, however, they added certain values their customers could use, in addition to holding down costs, CIGNA and Staples could sharpen their competitive edge.

Although well established and highly successful, Staples retail stores felt fierce pressure from competitors like Office Depot and OfficeMax. Rather than engage in risky price wars, Staples sought out intimacy with selected customers as a way of securing their long-term loyalty. Where did they start? Staples first amassed a huge database of customer information through its special discount card. By recategorizing this data, Staples created insightful profiles of the needs and purchasing habits of various individuals and professions. Lawyers and dentists, for example, are reliable, repeat buyers. By tailoring its operations to serve these customers, Staples was in a better position to decide where to place new stores, what types of services should be offered in different locales, and how best to control inventories and avoid overstocks and shortages for particular markets. The company was able to improve service inside stores, handle phone inquiries from outside more efficiently, and inspire a new degree of customer comfort and allegiance.

The company's ambitions for large *Fortune* 500 accounts led to the purchase in 1994 of National Office Supply, which managed office supplies for IBM and Ford Motor Company, among others. According to Ron Sargent, head of Staples' large-account and catalog business, National Office Supply was acquired for its managerial strength. "What we ended up valuing most was not National's operational skills per se, but the impact those skills had on the ability to meet specific customer demands, no matter how outlandish." Its operational flexibility and history of catering to demanding customers gave the company a distinct advantage in generating customized products and services. These features were incorporated into the newly formed Staples National Advantage (SNA), which built upon these skills to create a contract office supply company so customer intimate that customers today refer to SNA employees as "advocates."

The route from operational competence to customer intimacy is the most commonly traveled, perhaps because it implies functioning at a high level of productivity and efficiency. When all processes and systems are at peak levels of performance, any move—even one as major as the shift to intimacy—is bound to be less daunting. I have little doubt that operationally competent companies will continue to lead the pack of those moving toward customer intimacy.

Product Development Skills

Scania in Sweden and Johnson Controls Automotive in the United States moved to customer intimacy by designing superior products to the specific requirements of carefully selected companies and customers.

In business for more than 90 years, Scania has established a reputation for manufacturing trucks that are reliable, safe, cost-efficient, and environment-friendly. Facing increased competition from Mercedes and Volvo, Scania capitalized on its enviable reputation by making trucks according to requirements set by customers. What's more desirable than a top-quality truck? How about a top-quality truck designed to meet your needs exactly? The company worked with modular assembly plants to develop the most flexible and cost-efficient methods of production. Customers continue to buy Scania trucks because they are dependable and well made, but they are particularly pleased that the company can give them exactly what they need to make their businesses more efficient.

Johnson Controls Automotive makes more than a third of the seats that go into U.S. cars, manufactures private-label batteries for Sears and other retailers, and is a market leader in each of its various business segments. The company made its move to intimacy by going into its customers' plants and helping them redesign the processes in which they use these products.

Customer Affinity

Some companies stand out in the marketplace not because they offer excellent services and distinctive products, but because they clearly understand their customers' idiosyncratic needs. These companies have a deep affinity with their customers. They offer extensive consulting skills, an exceptional ability to manage change, or both. Their empathy with their customers gives them a predisposition to intimacy. And when the decision is made to take on the rigorous and demanding requirements of becoming truly customer intimate, these are the skills that companies rely on to enhance their market positions.

"We knew early on that customer service would be an important component of this business," says Ann Hayes Lee, senior vice president and COO of Calyx & Corolla. As we've seen, C&C went far beyond the usual offerings of customer service. The personal attention that the company gave to one of its customers was so extensive and appealing that the customer described the relationship as "like having tea with a good friend."

C&C used its 800 number to reach out to customers in ways that go far beyond the traditional mail-order services. Most companies report that the majority of calls received at their toll-free lines are "WISMOs": Where Is My Order? At C&C, customer-service reps receive sensitivity training that encourages them to act like consultants, even at times like interior decorators. Sure, they can tell you where your order is, but C&C has become so customer-intimate that it can now tell you the scent of a particular flower, the best way to care for it, the style of the bouquet and vase, and much more.

AutoZone established a reputation for consulting with car owners and backyard mechanics to find total solutions for their problems. The company bundled products and services for one-stop, customer-intimate results. This orientation to the specific requirements of customers gave AutoZone a distinct advantage in finding new ways to handle inventory, to offer uniform service at all outlets, and to make consumers feel more connected to the company.

Some insurance companies, such as Northwestern Mutual Life, tailor plans to individual needs spread over a lifetime. Some health providers, such as NovaCare, understand that "relationships determine results." These companies hone their competitive edge on the whetstone of detailed knowledge about their customers.

Brokering Talents

The fourth competence that I see as a sound starting point for intimacy is prowess in acting as a broker or general contractor—proficiency in taking on the role of assembling the various components of broad solutions. The strength of these companies lies in their network of contacts, their capacity to orchestrate the various components of change, and their ability to act as facilitators. These companies, like those discussed above, are already performing a prototypical customer-intimate function. Aggressively pursuing full-scale customer intimacy means using that function as the means to an end, not the end itself.

Degrémont, for example, has successfully established itself in several foreign countries—from the fjords of Norway to the Chinese hinterland—because it acted effectively as a broker with local businesses and institutions. This is especially true in less well-developed countries where Degrémont often helps its customers design and obtain the best financial solutions. Degrémont is the only profitable foreign company in the water-treatment business in Japan, largely because it worked with local coproviders to overcome seemingly insurmountable supply problems. Because it had acquired detailed knowledge of local businesses and cultures, Degrémont expanded its relationship with local contractors and scientists. Essentially it assumed the new role of coach or, in some cases, actually formed a partnership.

Value Call International is, by definition, a broker of various telecommunication options available from assorted suppliers. The company became customer intimate by honing this business function until it was able to address the specific needs of individuals and professions. Now VCI can put together packages of phone and fax services that satisfy needs—including some a customer might not even have been aware of having.

Just as some businesses with pronounced customer affinity might be tempted to think themselves already intimate with customers, those that engage in general contracting and brokering are likely to believe they're already delivering results and solutions. Only when brokering and contracting skills are put to use to find total solutions can a company truly practice customer intimacy. Companies with strong brokering skills, like those with customer affinity, should view their expertise as the starting point of their move to intimacy, not as an indication that they've already arrived.

None of the Above

Anyone serious about becoming customer intimate has to build a considerable amount of experience and expertise in at least one of these four areas. But what if none of the above applies in any significant way to your company right now? You don't have above-average operational competency or product development skills. Your customer affinity and brokering achievements aren't strong enough to serve as the foundation for intimacy. Does this leave you out in the cold? Not at all. There is another road to intimacy. It isn't as clearly directed as those we've detailed, but some of the most successful suppliers we've discussed in this book have used it as a means of reaching intimacy.

It's possible for a company to begin the challenging process of becoming customer intimate by focusing on only one or very few important customers at a time. With a manageable workload and the guidelines we've already outlined, the supplier can determine the exact nature of the customer's problems and its hierarchy of needs. What services are needed to bring about solutions? How should products be customized? In the process of answering these and other questions for one chosen customer, the supplier learns many of the competencies needed for intimacy—and moves on to the next customer. Thus, a company acquires the necessary skills through measured accretion to become fully customer intimate.

Nypro used its operational competence as a springboard into intimacy by building its customer-intimate skills gradually. In the 1980s, CEO Gordon Lankton decided to focus on a few, multimillion-dollar customers instead of a large number of smaller buyers. Gradually increasing its base of customers, Nypro learned the benefits and prerequisites of trust, coaching, partnering, and building solid relationships with customers. The company did not become a market leader overnight, but it learned from its experiences and built upon them—all with the clear goal of intimacy in mind. In its development of customer intimacy, Nypro represents a company that acquires skills and stacks them, one on top of the other, in order to reach its destination.

MAKE THE RIGHT MOVES

With a clear idea of where to begin the switch to customer intimacy, we now to turn to the question of how. You know your strengths, you know the area of expertise in which to look for starting points, but what turns will put you on the right road? Although no two companies that I've come to know have answered this question in the same way, the successful companies have initiated the transition with tactics that fall into one of three categories: revamping a core process, changing measurement and reward systems, and exercising customer selectivity.

Revamp a Core Process

Put in simple terms, this first move is redesigning a key process that affects how customers use your products and services. Redesign seeks to increase the total value of your offerings. It doesn't necessarily involve a major shift in technology, product development, or customer selectivity—although those might come later. What we're talking about here is changing a usage process as the lever to get intimacy off the ground.

CIGNA HealthCare revamped a core process as the first decisive action in becoming more customer intimate. Eric Chapman, regional director for CIGNA HealthCare's business service center in Phoenix, says, "Customers are looking for a health-care company that can give them hassle-free service—a company that knows them and appreciates their individual requirements. In becoming more customer intimate, we started from that premise."

The company looked at the way in which customers interacted with its sales- and service people. Typically, they dealt with individuals in different departments in different locations—billing, reconciliation, eligibility, enrollment, benefits, and member services. In order to establish one-on-one rapport with customers and assure them that someone who knew and cared about them was handling their problems, CIGNA switched to a "single point of contact," a system in which an "account specialist" was designated to handle all the concerns of a particular customer. "With a single point of contact," Chapman explains, "the customer works closely with the account specialist. They're not starting from scratch with each and every call."

This switch, which simplified life for the customer, was not without complications for the supplier. The new account specialists received an intimidating workload, and the customer service department found its old assumptions turned upside down. CIGNA minimized chaos by keeping focused on changes only to this core process. It didn't simultaneously make major changes in its incentive programs or its basic technology. Nor was customer selectivity a part of implementing this new approach. Mike Israelite, vice president, employer services for CIGNA HealthCare, says, "Everything we've done has amounted to organizing differently—around the customer. The people working the phones have the same tools they've always had. They're just using them differently."

CIGNA HealthCare's improvements have led to other moves and realignments, some of them even more dramatic. What's important to note here, however, is CIGNA's channeling the momentum from this initial maneuver.

Similarly, Samsung Electronics is creating a single point of contact in its Business Operations Center. According to manager Richard Choi, "We're changing the process first. In the beginning we don't even think about the system, we think about the vision: What's best for the customers? Our vision for the year 2000 is to answer any kind of question that a customer presents within two minutes and deliver within two days. Technology is only the tool. The relationships are the key."

Change Your Measurements and Rewards Systems

Whatever the merits of the maxim "Spare the rod and spoil the child," it's long been understood that people learn most effectively when they're given positive reinforcement and rewards. Incentive programs for employees, sales quotas, and performance-related bonuses can be invaluable tools for keeping a company jogging along at top speed. One way to get on the road to customer intimacy is to measure performance and hand out rewards in accordance with the goals of the discipline.

That's precisely the way Marshall Industries went from being customer friendly to being customer intimate. Robert Rodin, president and CEO, realized that Marshall's customer service was designed to make sales first and serve customers second. "Our people were shipping orders ahead of schedule so they could seal enough sales within a given period to win a prize. Customers want the order when they want it, not a week before. All of this 'We gotta score' attitude, this internal heat, was causing quality degradation, customer irritation, and, ultimately, increased costs. We knew the system had to be changed from the top. It would've been absurd to yell at someone for shipping ahead of schedule or distorting the system to hit the quotas when we were the ones who'd created the incentives."

Marshall eliminated all promotions and contests for all employees. It switched to profit sharing. Now, everyone receives a salary and a bonus based on the performance of the whole company—common goals instead of individual ones. This change has taken 600 salespeople off commission, virtually overnight. Since completing the program at the beginning of 1992, Marshall has grown from $575 million in sales to more than $1 billion—without commissions, incentives, promos, or contests. Costs have decreased from 18 percent to 11 percent, earnings have doubled, and the stock price has nearly tripled. The company became fully customer intimate. Changes in other processes and systems followed, but only after Marshall transformed the primary driver—metrics and rewards—by treating it as a measure of employees' collaborative efforts rather than one of individual performance.

Exercise Customer Selectivity

For many companies, the first step in becoming closer to important customers is phasing out burdensome relationships. Customer triage or selectivity can be the spearheading force to intimacy.

As we've seen, Nypro first put priority on only those accounts valued at $1 million or more. Airborne followed a similar path in focusing on high-volume corporate accounts such as Nike. Caliber Logistics carefully selected partners who value outsourcing, have an entrepreneurial corporate culture, and are willing to share risks. It views its technique as targeted sell, rather than mass sell.

NovaCare arranged its customers into a hierarchy of importance. Those customers with the greatest growth potential are designated blue chip. NovaCare focuses extraordinary resources on blue-chip facilities and programs. In the case of one such nursing home chain, business with NovaCare grew more than 30 percent in one year. Tim Foster, president and COO, notes the significance of this capability: "Had we not labeled that customer as being worthy of special recognition, it's doubtful we would have given it such focused attention and achieved such extraordinary growth."

Concentrating on one move to initiate the change can make the entire transformation to intimacy easier and more successful. Nypro's Gordon Lankton estimates that it took a few salespeople almost five years to understand and accept the concept of selecting— and sometimes refusing—customers. Some employees managed well; others had to leave the company. Targeting a single goal— selectivity—assured that the early stages of moving to intimacy did not create company-wide mayhem.

SHELTER FROM THE STORM

Doubters and saboteurs of intimacy lurk in the dark corners of nearly every company. Nothing incites suspicion and fear so quickly as the real and imagined threats inherent in change. The greater the change, the greater the fears.

To increase the chances for success, many of these companies have initiated their changes in sheltered, safe environments. Far from the potentially lethal meddling of naysayers, these courageous and sometimes fragile efforts at a revolutionary reconfiguration can grow in a nurturing environment.

CIGNA HealthCare's first moves toward intimacy were carried

out in an office in Phoenix, Arizona, far from its corporate nerve center in Hartford, Connecticut. ROLS was set up as a free-standing concern, separate from the rest of Roadway, whose employees might have been wary. When Procter & Gamble and Wal-Mart embarked on their historic partnership, teams from each company were located in an isolated Arkansas office. Many miles from their respective headquarters, they were free to forge a radically new model of working together.

The experiences of employees who've suffered under downsizing and reengineering prove that some fears are well-founded. Managers must acknowledge the legitimacy of some worries and show compassion to those in the company who aren't inclined toward bold steps. But while acknowledging concerns, a company must provide a healthy, protected space in which the shift to customer intimacy can commence.

THE COMMON GROUND

Every company begins from its own strengths and makes the initiating moves most appropriate for its own particular situation. Regardless of starting points and momentum-building moves, the companies I've studied have had two important traits in common: a sense of urgency about customer intimacy and an uplifting team spirit. The significance of these traits can't be underplayed. Think of them as the weather systems that dominate a company and create the environmental conditions conducive to customer intimacy. Trying to pursue the discipline without these traits is like trying to breathe in a vacuum.

A sense of urgency induces people to learn faster, correct mistakes more aggressively, and strive to find innovative applications. Urgency is not about rushing. It's about combining a determination to move ahead now and move ahead quickly with professionalism and care. A wait-and-see attitude will never carry you into the future on the crest of the wave. If something's worth striving for, it's worth striving for with fervor and zeal.

Leaders can and must lead, but employees from all ranks of a company—from the back office and the front—must participate in the shift to customer intimacy. A team spirit, a sense of shared goals, must light up a company's efforts at intimacy. Teams of people working together create more excitement, more energy, more ideas, and more enthusiasm than individuals ever can.

I began this study of customer intimacy by asking you to imagine several different companies and the almost unimaginable degree of closeness they've achieved with their customers. I'd like to end this book by asking you to enlist your imagination once again. But this time, I want you to think about your company and about yourself. Think about where you are right now. Think about your current position in the marketplace and your prospects for the future. What are your aspirations, your hopes, your dreams?

Now imagine a company courageous enough, bold enough, and forward-looking enough to accept the challenge of pursuing the most important business discipline the present has to offer the future. Imagine a company of urgent, energetic, team-spirited employees reaching out together and grasping for tomorrow's brightest promise. Imagine the unimaginable for your company, your employees, yourself.

Then open your eyes and get to work.

INDEX

ACKNOWLEDGMENTS

The premise of this book is that the success of customer-intimate firms is determined by their customers' results, and that to bolster customers' results, you have to know them intimately and work with them closely.

As such, I'm expanding on ideas expressed many years ago by Peter Drucker in his work *Managing for Results.* I'm also drawing on the insights of Ray Corey, Ted Levitt, and Ben Shapiro who inspired me at Harvard Business School in the late 1970s. It was there, in fact, that I first heard the term "customer intimacy." I salute these and other thought-leaders who have stimulated my thinking on this topic over the years: Phil Kotler, Len Schlesinger, and Lou Stern.

Customer intimacy as depicted in this book has its roots in the consulting work John Thompson and I did in the late 1980s on the subjects of channel strategy and the customer's experience cycle. Others who shaped my conception of close supplier–customer connections include Mike Hammer and Tom Peters.

In 1991, I introduced the topic of customer intimacy to the four dozen or so corporate sponsors of CSC/Index's Alliance research program. Their practical input, along with insights gained from a variety of consulting projects, helped to crystallize what became one of three disciplines that Michael Treacy and I (with Jay Michaud's research assistance) described in our *Harvard Business Review* article,

"Customer Intimacy and OtherValue Disciplines" (January–February, 1993). That article became the foundation for our book, *The Discipline of Market Leaders* (1995).

In *Customer Intimacy,* I'm expanding and evolving the themes of my earlier work. This book has benefited enormously from my ongoing exposure to leading practitioners. Many of them are featured in this work, many of them are not. I am grateful for their willingness to share experiences, engage in discussion, and provide access to their company and customers. To all of them I express heartfelt appreciation for their efforts to advance the frontier of customer value.

I would like to acknowledge several ex-colleagues at CSC/Index for their support, reactions, and ideas. They are Russell Brackett, Alan Budovitch, Karen Carper, Jim Champy, Ron Christman, Allen Cohen, Vince DiBianca, Lyn Goldman, Charlie Gottdiener, Gary Gulden, Jim Hall, Steve Hoffman, Saj-Nicole Joni, Jim Kennedy, Bob Linderman, Glenn Mangurian, Kirt Mead, Lou Peluso, Rhoda Pitcher, Brad Power, Martha Reedy, Dave Robinson, Judi Rosen, Greg Thorson, Greg Tucker, Tom Waite, Rick Wilson, and Walt Wilson.

Thanks also to my European friends and colleagues: François Austin, Michael Black, Bob Buday, Philippe Chenevière, Tony DiRomualdo, Jens-Marten Lohse, Laurent Marbacher, Anne Miller, Richard Pawson, Karlheinz Schwuchow, Robin Thompson, and Tony Tiernan.

I cannot imagine creating a book of this nature without the tailoring, coaching, and partnering efforts of a very special team of people. Thus, a special thank-you goes to Nelson Aldrich, Donna Sammons Carpenter, Curtis Hartman, Stephan McCauley, Sebastian Stuart, and the other talented writers, editors, and researchers at Wordworks, Inc.—Christina Braun, Maurice Coyle, Sara Delano, Elyse Friedman, Erik Hansen, Martha Lawler, Randi Purchia, Cindy Sammons, and Pat Wright. Thanks also to Helen Rees, my literary agent, and to Lorraine Spurge and her staff at Knowledge Exchange, my publisher, whose support and enthusiasm for this book knew no boundaries.

Finally, a thank-you goes to my wife Catherine for being a wonderful thought-partner, source of inspiration and sharp-eyed editor; and to my daughter Annelise, for being a great supporter.